Contains
110 CRAFT IDEAS

THE BIG BOOK OF BIBLE CRAFTS

Thoughtful

Polit

Kind

...lligent   Hardworking

Anna-Grace

Barnabas
for
Children®

Barnabas for Children® is a registered word mark and the logo is a registered
device mark of The Bible Reading Fellowship.

This edition copyright © BRF 2016
Illustrator: Jan Knudson
Cover photographer: Rebecca J Hall
Inside photographer: Rodney Stewart
The authors assert the moral right to be identified as the authors of this work

Published by
The Bible Reading Fellowship
15 The Chambers, Vineyard
Abingdon OX14 3FE
United Kingdom
Tel: +44 (0)1865 319700
Email: enquiries@brf.org.uk
Website: www.brf.owrg.uk
BRF is a Registered Charity

ISBN 978 0 85746 495 8

Originally published in the USA
by Group Publishing Inc. under the title
The Best of Children's Ministry Magazine: Crafts
Copyright © **2007** by **Group Publishing Inc.**

First UK edition published 2016
10 9 8 7 6 5 4 3 2 1 0
All rights reserved

Acknowledgements
Unless otherwise stated, scripture quotations are taken from The Holy Bible, New International Version
(Anglicised edition) copyright © 1973, 1978, 1984, 2011 by Biblica (formerly International Bible Society).
Used by permission of Hodder & Stoughton Publishers, an Hachette UK company. All rights reserved. 'NIV'
is a registered trademark of Biblica (formerly International Bible Society). UK trademark number 1448790.

Scripture quotations taken from the Holy Bible, New Living Translation, copyright © 1996, 2004, 2007, 2013.
Used by permission of Tyndale House Publishers, Inc., Carol Stream, Illinois 60188. All rights reserved.

A catalogue record for this book is available from the British Library

Printed by Gutenberg Press, Tarxien, Malta

THANKS TO OUR TALENTED AUTHORS!

Tracey Abney

Charlene Baker

Lynette Brown

Carolyn Caufman

Laurie Copley

Gay Correll

Mary J. Davis

Kelley Dean

Susan Dietrich

Kathleen Dowdy

Wave Dreher

Tom Fethe

Brooke Fisher

Joy Gerhart

Nanette Goings

Susan Grover

Debbie Gustafson

Sheila Halasz

Beverly Harman

Debbie Holford

Charlotte Inskeep

Ellen Javernick

Carmen Kamrath

Janel Kauffman

Andrea Kessler

Robyn Kundert

Betty Lentz

Nancy Lettardy

Neil MacQueen

Todd Medlin

Ruth Mooney

Judith Moy

Estha Murenbeeld

Amy Nappa

Cynthia Nelson

Wendy Nelson

Lori Niles

Debbie Trafton O'Neal

Leticia Parks

Terri Quillen

Jolene L. Roehlkepartain

Deborah Rowley

Tina Sagisi

RoseAnne Sather

Doris Schuchard

Beverly Schwind

Anabel Silveira

Julianne Winkler Smith

Sandy Spooner

Pat Sullivan

Sandra Thompson

Martha Turman

Mark von Ehrenkrook

Tina Vosberg

Joclyn Wampler

Gordon and Becki West

Terry Williams

Debbie Zachariah

CONTENTS

CRAFTS FOR YOUNGER CHILDREN (3–7s)

INDEX

123

CONTENTS

INTRODUCTION

It's been said that you just can't do children's ministry without crafts.

That's why we've taken 110 of the best craft ideas from *Children's Ministry Magazine* and put them all into one easy-to-use book. Gleaned from issues spanning ten years, these creative crafts are not only fun, but also easy to do.

A wide variety of children's ministry experts have contributed these craft ideas, so we know they work. Helpful illustrations mean you'll never have to guess the next step. Indexes make it possible to search by the scripture reference or season in the year, so finding the perfect craft will be easy!

Use this collection of craft ideas

• to find crafts for your next special event,

• to fill in the gaps of your curriculum,

• as a resource to help volunteers in their planning, and

• as an instant resource when you need an instant craft

Keep this book to hand—you'll use it often! It's a craft lifesaver for Sunday school, midweek groups and holiday clubs.

Now get crafty!

PLEASE NOTE

Children's abilities differ, so always make sure you are satisfied the activity is appropriate and safe for the children in your care.

When taking photos of children, it is essential to obtain parental permission.

CRAFTS FOR

ALL AGES

ANGEL POP ORNAMENTS

Kids can make these fun ornaments to set in their Christmas tree branches, and then eat the lollipop after Christmas.

WHAT YOU'LL NEED:

You'll need a lollipop, 2 white tissues, white string, a 15 cm square of yellow tissue paper and gold tinsel for each ornament. You'll also need felt-tip pens and glue. (Boiled-sweet lollipops can be a choking hazard for younger children so chocolate ones may be more suitable for them.)

FOR EXTRA IMPACT:

- Read aloud **Luke 2:8–14**, and let the children act out the story. They can take turns being shepherds and angels.

- Ask the children why they think the shepherds were afraid.

- Let them take turns sharing about a time when they were afraid and someone comforted them.

WHAT TO DO

Place the centre of the white tissues over the lollipop, gather the tissues around the base of the sweet, and tie with string. Scrunch the yellow tissue-paper square in the centre, glue the centre of the square to the back of the tissue-covered sweet, and fan out the ends of the square to form the angel wings.

Next, glue a small circle of gold tinsel to the top of the lollipop as a halo, and decorate the angel's face with felt-tip pens. Tie string around the angel's 'neck', forming a loop to use as a Christmas tree hanger.

ALLERGY ALERT

Be aware that some children have food allergies that can be dangerous. Know your children, and consult with parents about any allergies that their children may have. Also, be sure to read food labels carefully as hidden ingredients can cause allergy-related problems.

ANIMAL ARKY

Kids learn about Noah's ark with this cooperative craft.

WHAT YOU'LL NEED:

You'll need 2 large boxes, brown parcel-wrapping paper or similar, yellow and grey acrylic paint, sturdy cardboard, white, yellow, pink, orange and black card, white, yellow, orange and black poster paint, paintbrushes, orange sugar paper, coat-hanger wire, glue (a hot-glue gun would be useful, for adult use only), clear packaging tape, scissors, a ruler, newspapers and painting shirts.

FOR EXTRA IMPACT:

- Paraphrase **Genesis 6–9**.
- Let the children colour a large box as an ark, then act out the story of Noah.

WHAT TO DO

Cover your work area with newspapers, and give children painting shirts. Help the children paint and decorate the animals.

For the elephant—Cover the box with the parcel paper, then paint it with grey acrylic paint. Using sturdy cardboard, cut out one giant heart for the head and two medium-size hearts for the ears. Paint these grey. Cut out pink card hearts for the inside of the ears and stick them in place. Using black card, cut out two hearts for the eyes, a 25 cm tail and 30 cm tusks. Cut out two 5 cm x 70 cm pieces of card for the trunk. Paint these grey. Then curve a coat-hanger wire and tape it between the two pieces so it will appear that the trunk is curved. Tape the trunk together. Glue all the items to the box and reinforce them with clear packaging tape.

For the giraffe—Cover the box with parcel paper, then paint it yellow. Roll a sheet of yellow card into a tube for the giraffe's neck, and tape it. Glue fringed orange sugar paper to the giraffe's neck. Using sturdy cardboard, cut out one heart-shaped head, and paint it yellow. From the coloured card, cut out smaller hearts for the giraffe's ears, mouth and eyes. Cut out its antlers and tail, and patches for its body. Cut a neck hole in the box and insert the neck. Glue the items to the box and reinforce them with tape.

BABY MOSES BASKETS

Kids love making these edible treats as they learn about Moses.

WHAT YOU'LL NEED:

You'll need Shredded Wheat® cereal or cornflakes, milk chocolate, a microwave and bowl for melting the chocolate, mixing bowls, dessert spoons, cake cases, jelly beans and red liquorice laces.

ALLERGY ALERT

See page 10.

FOR EXTRA IMPACT:

- Roll out some blue fondant icing or use blue cardboard. Place the basket on top of the blue 'water'.

- Read aloud **Exodus 2:1–10** as the children eat their snacks.

- Read aloud **Mark 6:30–44**. Ask the children to fill their baskets with jelly beans ('fish') and small pieces of bread to represent Jesus feeding the 5000.

WHAT TO DO

Ask the children to wash their hands, then form small groups and work together to make baskets. Place the Shredded Wheat® cereal or cornflakes in a bowl. Ask an adult to melt the chocolate, then pour the melted chocolate over the cereal and ask the children to mix it together using the dessert spoons.

The children can then spoon the mixture into the cake cases, pressing the spoon down in the centre of each one to make a 'basket'.

Use a piece of red liquorice lace to form a handle and attach it by sticking it into the top sides of the basket. Put a jelly bean in each basket to represent baby Moses.

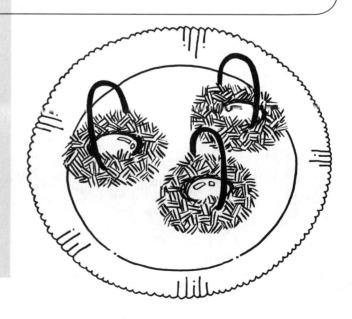

BALAAM'S DONKEY

Kids learn about Balaam's experience with these cute talking donkeys.

WHAT YOU'LL NEED:

You'll need a Bible, brown paper bags (or if you can't find these, pieces of card folded in half so they can stand up), pink paint, paint brushes, card, wool, large googly eyes, scissors, glue and miniature marshmallows.

FOR EXTRA IMPACT:

- Ask the children: have you ever been told off? How did you feel?

- Ask: why does God want us to obey his commands?

- Read aloud **Colossians 3:20**. Ask the children why it pleases God when we obey our parents.

WHAT TO DO

Cut the donkey's face and ears from the card. Glue these and the googly eyes to the paper bag. Use wool to make the donkey's reins and mane. Paint the inside of the donkey's mouth with pink paint and glue on marshmallow teeth. (Remind the children not to eat the marshmallows after they've come into contact with the glue!)

Read aloud **Numbers 22:21–34**. Then say: when Balaam's donkey wouldn't obey him because it saw the angel of God, Balaam became very angry and scolded it. When God let the donkey speak, it asked Balaam why he'd got so angry. Then God opened Balaam's eyes so he could see the angel standing in the way. Balaam finally understood why his donkey wouldn't obey him.

Ask: how do you think Balaam's donkey felt when it was being scolded? What did Balaam learn from his experience?

ALL AGES

BEADED BOOKMARKS

Kids make festive bookmarks as a reminder of our different gifts.

WHAT YOU'LL NEED:

You'll need waxed jewellery cord, medium-size mixed beads, decorative card, a ruler, a hole punch, scissors and decorative pens.

FOR EXTRA IMPACT:

- Read aloud **Romans 12:4–8**, and ask the children why God gives each of us different gifts. Ask: how should we use those gifts?

- Ask the children to find a partner and talk about their different gifts.

- Get the children to write on an index card one gift they feel they have, then lay all the cards out on a table, and look at all the different gifts. Close in prayer, thanking God for the many gifts he gives us.

WHAT TO DO

Cut a 30 cm length of jewellery cord. Cut a piece of card 2.5 cm x 5 cm and punch a hole in one corner. Write, '"We have different gifts, according to the grace given to each of us"—Romans 12:6' on one side of the card. Thread the card on to the cord as a gift tag.

Tie a double knot 5 cm from each end of the piece of cord. Choose any combination of beads and thread them on to both ends of the cord to the knots. Tie off each end as close to the base of the beads as possible. Clip off any extra cord.

BERRY SPECIAL

Kids have fun creating this gift for people they love.

WHAT YOU'LL NEED:

You'll need red felt, green felt, hair clips (jaw-clip style), fine-tipped permanent markers, glue, scissors, an instant-print camera and enough instant-print film to take a photo of each child.

FOR EXTRA IMPACT:

- Ask the children: how can we make other people feel special? Why is it important to make others feel special?

- Let the children talk about something special that someone has done for them.

- Ask the children to sit in a circle and throw a ball back and forth while shouting, 'You're berry special!' until the leader yells, 'Stop!' The child who catches the ball should say something special about the last child to throw the ball and then continue throwing the ball around the circle.

WHAT TO DO

Provide a strawberry pattern that children can trace four times on to their red felt. As each child traces the strawberry shapes, take photos of the other children until you have a photo of everyone. Ask the children to hold up a sign that says, 'You're berry special!' as their photos are taken.

Use a fine-tipped marker to dot the 'seeds' on to each strawberry. Glue two felt strawberries together, covering one side of the hair clip between them. Then repeat the procedure with the other side of the hair clip.

Cut out strawberry leaves from the green felt and glue them to the top of the strawberries. Clip each child's strawberry clip to his or her photo. The children can sign their names on the blank spaces under their photos.

YOU'RE BERRY SPECIAL!

Eriko

BETHLEHEM STAR

Kids can use this easy-to-make craft as an ornament or gift.

WHAT YOU'LL NEED:

You'll need cardboard, scissors, yellow felt, glitter glue and candy canes. Cut star patterns (see below right) from cardboard.

FOR EXTRA IMPACT:

- Read aloud **Matthew 2:1–3, 7–12**, and ask the children why the magi were so excited to see the star. Ask: how do you think you might have felt?

- Let the children decorate a classroom tree with their star ornaments.

- Get the children to cover star-shaped biscuits with yellow icing and top with sprinkles for a stellar snack.

ALLERGY ALERT

See page 10.

WHAT TO DO

Trace the cardboard patterns on to yellow felt and cut out the stars. Fold the long piece along the dotted lines, and cut along the dotted lines. Weave the shorter piece through the slits in the long piece.

Use glitter glue to decorate the star. Then lay the star flat to dry. Once the star is dry, stick a candy cane through its back to hang on a Christmas tree.

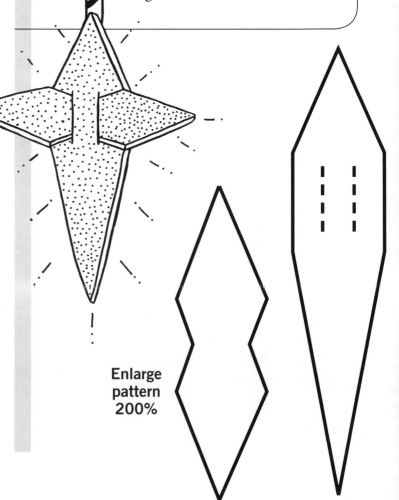

Enlarge pattern 200%

BIG FISH SOCKS

Kids create colourful praise windsocks.

WHAT YOU'LL NEED:

You'll need coloured tissue paper, sugar paper, wool, scissors, pipe cleaners, a hole punch, glue, clear sticky tape and 60 cm-long dowel rods.

FOR EXTRA IMPACT:

- Bring in a fan, and let the children test their windsocks. If it's a windy day, take them outside.

- Read aloud **Psalm 8**, and ask the children why we praise the Lord.

- Sit in a circle. Let the children stand up one at a time, name something they're thankful for, wave their windsock and shout, 'Lord, you're the king!'

WHAT TO DO

Before the children arrive, draw a fish pattern to fit on a large sheet of tissue paper. Cut two tissue-paper fish for each child from the pattern. Mark the holes as shown on the pattern below. Cut two sugar-paper fins for each child.

For each fish, ask the children to cover both sides of the mouth with clear sticky tape to reinforce it, leaving the mouth open. Punch holes along the mouth.

Glue one fin along the top edge of the fish body and one fin along the bottom edge. Glue the two fish together around the edges, leaving the mouth and tail area open to allow the windsock to fill with air and the air to escape out of the tail.

When the glue is dry, weave one pipe cleaner in and out of the holes, forming a circle. Tie wool through each hole. Tie the ends of the wool together at one end of a wooden dowel, and glue them in place. Children can carry their Big Fish Socks on a windy day.

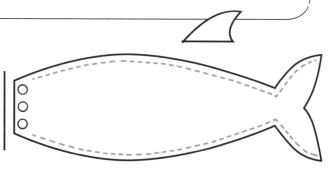

BIRDS DON'T WORRY

Kids make these fun edible birds' nests to remember that God cares for them.

WHAT YOU'LL NEED:

You'll need Shredded Wheat® cereal or cornflakes, milk chocolate, a microwave and bowl for melting the chocolate, mixing bowls, dessert spoons, cake cases and mini chocolate eggs or jelly beans. You'll also need a Bible.

ALLERGY ALERT

See page 10.

FOR EXTRA IMPACT:

• Teach the children this rhyme to help them to remember **Matthew 6:25–26**:

Don't worry about what you eat, drink or wear.

Trust in God like the birds of the air.

• Ask them: how do you feel knowing you don't have to worry because you can trust God for all things?

• Close in prayer, and let each child thank God for one thing.

WHAT TO DO

Ask the children to wash their hands. Pour the cereal into the mixing bowls. Ask an adult to melt the chocolate, then pour this over the cereal and let the children mix the ingredients together. Spoon the mixture into cake cases then flatten down the centre to create a 'nest'. Place three mini chocolate eggs in each nest to represent birds' eggs, or use jelly beans or similar sweets to represent young birds.

As the children eat their 'nests', encourage them to talk about things they worry about. Assure them of God's provision and care for them by reminding them of **Matthew 6:25–26**. Explain that God takes care of the birds, and he'll take even more care of them.

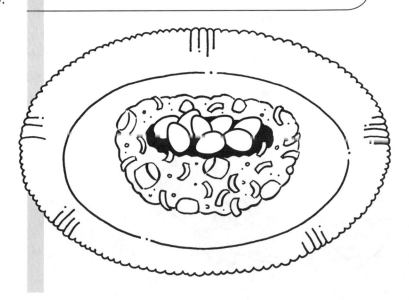

BLESSING BIRDS

Kids encourage one another with this fun craft.

WHAT YOU'LL NEED:

You'll need 1 pine cone, 1 brown pom-pom, 2 small googly eyes, and 7 'feathers' for each bird, precut from thin card. You'll also need red and orange sugar paper, felt-tip pens, PVA glue and scissors.

FOR EXTRA IMPACT:

- Read aloud **Philemon 1:4**, and encourage the children to pray for their friends every day.

- Encourage the children to think of someone they're thankful for and to explain how that person makes them feel special.

WHAT TO DO

Ask each child to glue a brown pom-pom to the top of the small end of a pine cone. This is the turkey's head. Glue googly eyes to the pom-pom head. Cut red sugar paper to make the wattle (the fold of skin hanging from the head) and orange sugar paper for the beak. Glue these on to the pom-pom head.

Ask the children to write their name on a 'feather', dab the bottom edge of the feather with glue and insert it at the back of their pine-cone turkey and into its spines.

Get the children to form a circle and pass their turkeys around it. When children get a turkey, ask them to write an affirming word about the turkey's owner on to a feather. They should then dab glue on the bottom edge of the feather and insert it into that child's turkey.

As the turkeys dry, ask children to share some of the things they wrote. Close in prayer, thanking God for each child in your group.

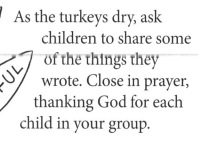

BUTTERFLY AND CROSS SALT-DOUGH ORNAMENTS

Kids love celebrating Easter with these festive ornaments.

WHAT YOU'LL NEED:

You'll need resealable plastic food bags, flour, salt, water, rolling pins, cups, cross and butterfly cookie cutters, watercolour paints, paintbrushes, glue, sequins, wool or ribbon, scissors, buttons, glitter, a foil-covered baking tray and an oven.

ALLERGY ALERT

See page 10.

FOR EXTRA IMPACT:

• Let the children make extra cross ornaments. Spread with vegetable shortening and cover with birdseed, then take home to hang in a tree for an Easter celebration the birds will love.

WHAT TO DO

Ask the children to form groups of four and decide which task they want to do, such as measure the flour, salt or water, or mix the dough. In a resealable food bag, mix 1 cup of flour and 1 cup of salt. Add half a cup of water, a little at a time. Squeeze the bag to mix thoroughly, then remove the dough, and form into a ball. (With so much salt added, remind the children not to eat any of the mixture!)

Divide the dough into four pieces. Knead each piece until smooth, then roll it out to about 0.5 cm thick on a lightly floured surface. Cut with butterfly and cross cookie cutters. Make a small hole at the top of each cut-out. Bake the cut-outs on a foil-covered baking tray at 170°C (150°C fan) until golden brown, or air-dry for 48 hours or until hard.

At the next session, paint the hardened cut-outs with watercolours. Use glue to decorate with sequins, buttons and glitter. Thread wool or ribbon through the hole at the top and hang.

Ask the children: why do crosses and butterflies remind us of Easter? Why do we celebrate Easter? How does your family celebrate Easter?

BUTTERFLY WINGS

Kids learn about becoming new creations in Christ.

WHAT YOU'LL NEED:

You'll need clear self-adhesive covering film (the type used to cover books), masking tape, glitter, sequins, a permanent marker, craft lollipop sticks, pipe cleaners, brown paper bags, scissors and glue or sticky tape.

FOR EXTRA IMPACT:

- Make butterfly-wing patterns out of card, so the children can draw round these on their creations to help them cut the butterfly shape.

- Read aloud **2 Corinthians 5:17**, and discuss what it means to be a new creation in Christ.

- Ask the children to remove their butterflies from their paper-bag cocoons and discuss how that is or isn't like what happens to people when they become new creations in Christ.

WHAT TO DO

Cut a square of self-adhesive film for each child. Peel the backing off the film and tape the edges to the table using masking tape, with the sticky side up. Ask the children to decorate the sticky side of their film with glitter and sequins, then help them lay another piece of sticky film over their creations. Let the children cut their creation into a butterfly shape. Glue or tape a lollipop stick to the centre of the butterfly for the body, and a pipe cleaner to the stick for the antennae. Add a mouth and eyes with the permanent marker.

Ask the children to put their butterflies into brown paper bags to resemble cocoons. Tell them that a caterpillar lives its life on the ground and then makes a cocoon where it seems to die. But the caterpillar isn't dead; a miracle is happening in the cocoon, and the caterpillar is turning into a butterfly.

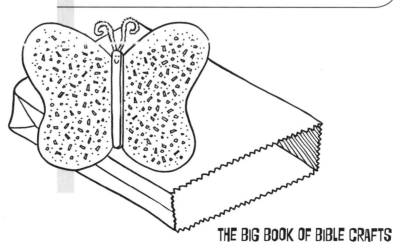

BUTTERMILK 'MIRACLES'

Kids learn that miracles are possible with God.

WHAT YOU'LL NEED:

You'll need buttermilk in a bowl, 2.5 cm-wide foam brushes, pastel-coloured sugar paper, coloured chalk and a Bible. Cover the table with a vinyl cloth, or have a sponge handy to wipe the table when you're finished.

ALLERGY ALERT

See page 10.

FOR EXTRA IMPACT:

- Keep an ongoing prayer chart, and list children's prayer requests. As the prayers are answered, mark them on the prayer chart as a visible reminder of God's power.

- Share a time with the children when God answered one of your prayer requests with a 'no'. Reassure them that we can always trust God to answer our prayers according to his purposes.

WHAT TO DO

Read aloud **John 2:1–11**. Encourage the children to dip the sponge brushes in buttermilk and smear buttermilk on the sugar paper. Make sure children cover the entire page.

Next ask the children to draw a picture with the coloured chalk directly on to the wet buttermilk surface. The buttermilk will keep the chalk drawing from smearing or smudging. Set aside to dry.

Ask: did you think you would be able to draw on the wet buttermilk? Why, or why not? Did the people at the wedding believe that Jesus could turn water into wine? Why, or why not? What is a miracle?

Say: God can work miracles in your life even when it seems impossible. What are some miracles we need to ask God to do in our lives?

Close in prayer, asking God to work a miracle in the areas children mention.

CATERPILLAR TO BUTTERFLY MOBILES

Kids make colourful mobiles to remind them of the way God transforms us.

WHAT YOU'LL NEED:

You'll need 2 wooden-doll pegs for each child, poster paint, paintbrushes, tissue paper, glitter, glue, scissors, pipe cleaners, wool and pencils.

FOR EXTRA IMPACT:

- Bring in actual cocoons and butterflies or photographs for the children to see.

- Read aloud **Mark 16:4–8**, and ask: how is Jesus' resurrection like or unlike the caterpillars changing to butterflies?

WHAT TO DO

For the caterpillar, cut one pipe cleaner into thirds. Form legs by folding each third into a U-shape. Bend the tips out for feet. Arrange the legs between the prongs of one doll peg, and secure them with dots of glue. Decorate the caterpillar with paint and pipe-cleaner antennae.

For the butterfly, fold two layers of tissue paper in a concertina style. Wedge the tissue paper between the prongs of the doll peg, centring it. Spread the layers to create butterfly wings. Secure the wings with glue on each side.

Decorate the butterfly's wings by dabbing them with glue and applying glitter. Paint the butterfly's body. Make antennae by curling half-lengths of pipe cleaner around a pencil and attaching them to the butterfly's head with glue.

Use wool to string the caterpillar and butterfly together once they've dried. You can hang the mobiles in your meeting space or send them home with the children.

CHRISTMAS CONE

Kids will love making these gift cones for their families for Christmas.

WHAT YOU'LL NEED:

You'll need 20 cm squares of sugar paper or card, 5 cm x 25 cm strips of tissue paper, 25 cm lengths of ribbon, stickers, glue, scissors and individually wrapped sweets.

ALLERGY ALERT

See page 10.

FOR EXTRA IMPACT:

- Read aloud **Matthew 2:10–11**, and ask how Mary might have felt when the wise men gave baby Jesus gifts.

- Encourage the children to share how it feels to give gifts and how it feels to receive gifts.

- Ask: why do we give gifts? Let the children choose a special person to give their Christmas Cone to and tell the group who they chose and why.

WHAT TO DO

Roll the square into a cone shape, and glue the overlapping edges of the sugar paper/card together. Trim the excess paper/card to make the wide end of the cone level. Glue the tissue paper inside the cone 2 or 3 cm from the top, with the remaining tissue paper sticking above the edge. Decorate the cone with stickers. Fill the cone with sweets and tie the tissue paper with a ribbon.

CHRISTMAS WALL HANGING

Kids create this wall hanging as a Christmas keepsake.

WHAT YOU'LL NEED:

For each wall hanging you'll need a rectangle of white cotton fabric 50 cm x 90 cm, a 60 cm wooden dowel (2.5 cm in diameter) and a 90 cm red ribbon. You'll also need painting aprons, green, red and yellow poster paint, pinking shears and a hot-glue gun (adult use only). Have a supply of baby wipes ready for cleaning hands.

FOR EXTRA IMPACT:

- Create a bulletin board by letting the children paint their handprints to create a large tree. They can decorate the tree and write their names on their handprints.

- Ask the children to share their favourite Christmas memories.

- Let them sing their favourite Christmas carols and march around the room carrying their hangings.

WHAT TO DO

Before the children arrive, use pinking shears to trim all the edges of the fabric to prevent fraying. Outline a base for a tree at the bottom of the fabric with yellow paint. Using the red paint, write in the child's name and the year.

Let the children each dip their hands one at a time in green paint and place their handprints on their fabric to create the tree. Encourage them to make four to five handprints across the bottom, working up to only one handprint at the top, to form the tree. Decorate the tree by painting a yellow star on top and adding 'lights' with the red and yellow paint. Allow to dry.

Place a wooden dowel at the top edge of the hanging. Fold the edge of the fabric down around the dowel to the back of the hanging and get an adult to glue it into place. Tie the ribbon on to both ends of the dowel. Glue the ribbon to the dowel to create a hanger.

CHRISTMAS WREATH

Kids make colourful wreaths to decorate their fridges at home.

WHAT YOU'LL NEED:

You'll need plastic dessert plates, cling film, PVA glue, magnets, red ribbon and an old 500- or 1000-piece jigsaw puzzle. Several days before the activity, spray-paint three-quarters of the puzzle pieces green and the remaining pieces red. Allow these to dry.

FOR EXTRA IMPACT:

- Encourage the children to share the ways their families celebrate Christmas.

- Let them make wreaths to give to neighbours or friends. They can colour Christmas cards to give along with the wreaths.

- Use extra puzzle pieces and let the children make holly leaves and berries.

WHAT TO DO

Cover a plastic dessert plate with a piece of cling film. Lay several green puzzle pieces around the inner circle of the dessert plate. Overlap the puzzle piece edges, and glue the pieces together in the circle. Continue this process with two layers of green pieces on top of the first layer, with all layers glued together. Glue several red pieces here and there on the green pieces to resemble holly berries. Glue on a bow made from the red ribbon.

Allow the pieces to dry thoroughly. Then carefully peel the wreath from the cling film. Trim away any excess cling film. Attach a magnet to the back of the wreath so the children can hang their creations on their fridges at home.

CINNAMON ORNAMENTS

Kids make these ornaments to express love to their mothers.

WHAT YOU'LL NEED:

You'll need a Bible, 1 cup of ground cinnamon, mixing spoon, 1½ to 2 cups of flour, 2 cups of water, medium saucepan, hob, rolling pins, pencils and lengths of fishing line.

FOR EXTRA IMPACT:

- Get the children to sit in a circle and throw a beanbag or ball back and forth. As they catch the ball, they should shout ways they can honour their mothers.

- Challenge the children to pick their favourite way and honour their mother with that action during the week.

- Let the children decorate paper bags with markers, stickers and ribbons. They can use these to wrap their ornaments after they've dried.

WHAT TO DO

Before the children arrive, boil the water in the saucepan. Remove from the heat and stir in the cinnamon. Add the flour half a cup at a time and stir well. Knead the last half cup of flour into the dough after it has cooled slightly. Keep the dough in a container with a tight lid.

Let the children lightly flour a work area and roll out a piece of dough. They can mould it into a shape that reminds them of their mother, such as a heart, a smile or a helping hand. Use a pencil to make a hole at the top of the shape. String fishing line through the hole and tie a knot to make a hanger. Tell the children to take their ornaments home and let them dry for one to two days, then give them to their mother, grandmother or another special person so she can enjoy its fragrance.

Read aloud **Ephesians 6:2**. Ask: what does it mean to honour your mother? Why does God want us to honour our mothers? How can you honour your mother?

ALLERGY ALERT
See page 10.

CONTAINER CREATURES

Kids learn that God looks at the heart.

WHAT YOU'LL NEED:

You'll need an opaque container with sweets or treats inside, empty cylinder-shaped cardboard containers (such as Pringles® tubes), sugar paper, felt-tip pens, 30 cm pieces of thin rope or twine, large wooden beads or empty thread spools, pom-poms, glue or sticky tape and scissors.

FOR EXTRA IMPACT:

- Read aloud **1 Samuel 16:7**, and ask: why do we often judge people by the way they look on the outside? Why does God look at our hearts?

- Let the children fill their containers with sweets to remind them that God sees what's on the inside.

See page 10.

WHAT TO DO

Hold up the container with treats inside. Say: would you rather have this container or what's inside it? Explain.

Show the group what's inside the container. Say: containers are important, but they're not as important as what they hold inside. How is that like or unlike us? How can we learn to see a person's heart and not just the outside?

Ask children to wrap the empty containers with sugar paper. They can make a fun face with felt-tip pens, sugar paper and pom-poms for noses.

To make the legs, get an adult to use scissors to punch two small holes about 2 cm from the bottom edge and about 6 cm apart, under the face. Thread a 30 cm piece of thin rope or twine in one hole and out the other; pull it through until equal amounts of rope hang out of each hole. Tape the rope on the inside of the container to secure it. Tie a wooden bead or spool at each end of the rope for feet.

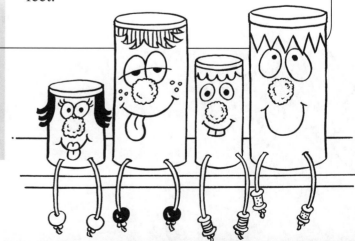

COTTON-WOOL VALENTINES

Kids will love this cooperative activity to make fun valentines.

WHAT YOU'LL NEED:

You'll need cotton-wool balls, red sugar paper, pens, scissors, envelopes, glue and spray perfume. Have extra collage materials on hand, such as wiggly eyes, pom-poms, wool, tissue paper and pipe cleaners.

FOR EXTRA IMPACT:

- Ask older children to write short verses of scripture inside the cards.

- Ask the children to share ways God shows his love for us.

- Let them choose a special group to send their cards to, such as nursing-home residents.

WHAT TO DO

Get the children to work together to form an assembly line. Let younger children do the glueing while older children draw and write. Work together to produce these cotton-wool valentine cards, starting with a sheet of red sugar paper folded in half:

'We love ewe!'—Use cotton-wool balls for a lamb's body. Draw the head and feet. Add wiggly eyes for a fun touch.

'You're sweet!'—Spray a cotton-wool ball 'flower' with perfume, and glue it on to a pipe cleaner. Draw or cut out tissue-paper petals to add to the flower.

'Our love for you will never end!'—Use a cotton-wool ball for a rabbit's tail. Add a miniature pom-pom for the bunny nose and make wool whiskers.

'We love you beary much!'—Use cotton-wool balls for a bear's tummy and head. Use miniature pom-poms for ears and paws. Glue on wiggly eyes.

Encourage the children to think up more ideas. When you have finished, place the cards in the envelopes, then ask the children to give them to a loved one.

DANDY LIONS

Kids create a tangible reminder that God's love helps them overcome their fears.

WHAT YOU'LL NEED:

You'll need paper plates, wool, yellow and brown sugar paper or thin card, a ruler, glue, scissors, black face paint and brushes, and a hole punch. You will also need a Bible.

FOR EXTRA IMPACT:

- Let the children wear their masks and act out the story of Daniel in the lions' den. They can take turns playing Daniel.

- Teach them this rhyme to say as they leave the lions' den.

  The lions did not hurt me;
  I was lifted from the den.

  I can trust in God
  again and again.

- For a tasty lion snack, cover cupcakes with yellow icing. Add orange Smarties® or jelly beans around the edge for the mane, use brown Smarties® for eyes and red liquorice laces for whiskers.

ALLERGY ALERT

See page 10.

WHAT TO DO

Cut out the centre of a white paper plate. Cut several 2.5 cm x 10 cm strips of yellow sugar paper or card. Apply the strips with glue, covering the perimeter of the plate to create a lion's mane. Cut out two brown ears, and glue them on top of the yellow mane. Punch a hole on each side of the plate, and tie a 25 cm piece of wool through each hole.

Ask the children to put their masks on, then line up to get their faces painted (if they want to!) with a black nose and whisker dots.

Read aloud **Daniel 6:16–23**. Then ask: how do you think Daniel felt when he was trapped in the lions' den? What would you have done? Why did God keep the lions from hurting Daniel? When you're afraid, how can you trust God the way Daniel did?

DAVID AND SAUL

Kids learn how Jesus wants us to treat our enemies.

WHAT YOU'LL NEED:

You'll need a Bible, felt-tip pens or crayons, sugar paper, scissors, glue and masking tape. Before the session, cut a 'robe' from a roll of paper.

FOR EXTRA IMPACT:

- Ask the older children to draw and cut out several hand outlines and then write on each one a different way they can be kind to others.

- Let the children find a partner and share their helping hand ideas with each other.

- Bring in some old dressing gowns, and let the children act out the story of David and Saul.

WHAT TO DO

Let the children use felt-tip pens or crayons to decorate the robe. Then tape it to the wall with the hem at floor level.

Paraphrase the story from **1 Samuel 24**. Then ask each child to sneak up as quietly as David did and cut off a small piece from the bottom of the robe. Draw around each child's hand on sugar paper. Then get the children to glue their robe remnant to their outlined hand.

Write a paraphrase of **1 Samuel 24:11** on each child's sheet of sugar paper. For example, 'A piece of your robe is in my hand, but I did not harm you.'

Ask the children: has anyone ever made you angry? Tell us about it. Did you ever want to hurt someone who hurt you?

Say: King Saul wanted to hurt David. King Saul was an enemy to David, but David treated King Saul kindly. Listen to what Jesus says he wants us to do to our enemies.

From an easy-to-understand translation, read aloud **Luke 6:27–31**.

Ask: why does God want us to be kind to all people? How can we be kind to people who are mean to us?

Close in prayer, asking God to help us to be kind to people even when they are mean.

"The skirt of your robe is in my hand and yet I did not harm you." 1 Sam. 24:11

EASTER EGG PIÑATA

Kids love making this festive craft to celebrate Easter.

WHAT YOU'LL NEED:

You'll need an inflated and tied-off balloon, dozens of newspaper strips (approximately 5 cm x 20 cm) and a 5 cm x 25 cm cardboard strip for each child. You'll also need a craft knife (adult use only), paint, paintbrushes, individually wrapped sweets, string, duct tape, a stapler, a thin mixture of plaster of Paris in an open container, newspapers, towels for cleaning up, a hairdryer, and painting shirts.

FOR EXTRA IMPACT:

- Ask the children to share the ways their families celebrate Easter.

- Read aloud **Luke 24:45–47**, and discuss the real meaning of Easter.

WHAT TO DO

Cover your work area with newspapers. Staple a cardboard strip into a 'crown' and place one under each balloon to help it stand up. Get the children to dip a newspaper strip into the plaster of Paris and then remove the excess mixture by running the strip between their index and middle fingers. Show them how to lay their lightly coated strip on their balloon and smooth it down so it lies flat. Repeat this process until the entire balloon is covered by two layers of strips. Help the children achieve uniformity in covering their balloons for the best results.

Allow the balloons to dry for one week. Then cut two small holes in the top of each balloon and remove the balloon fragments. At the next session, let the children paint the outside of their balloon shells, and allow the paint to dry. A hairdryer speeds up the drying time.

Give the children sweets to put into their piñatas, tie a string through the opening in the top, then stick duct tape over the opening. Let the children take their piñatas home and enjoy batting them until they break.

ALLERGY ALERT

See page 10.

EDIBLE MANGER SCENES

Kids will enjoy making this edible nativity scene.

WHAT YOU'LL NEED:

You'll need a Bible, rectangular biscuits or crackers, animal biscuits, jelly babies, Shredded Wheat® cereal, chocolate stars, miniature pretzels, marshmallows, one 20 cm x 25 cm piece of cardboard for each child, foil, plastic knives and icing sugar.

FOR EXTRA IMPACT:

- Ask the children to get into pairs and take turns retelling the Christmas story using their manger scenes.

- Encourage the children to design a manger scene, drawing around cookie cutters to make animals and people.

See page 10.

WHAT TO DO

Ask the children to wash their hands. Wrap the cardboard in foil to use as a base. Mix the icing sugar with a small amount of water to make a thick paste. Using this as 'glue', form a biscuit 'stable' on the base. Build three walls, then add the roof.

Add people and animals to the scene. Crumble Shredded Wheat® to add hay. Use the icing to attach a marshmallow to the centre of a pretzel to make an angel. Glue the angel and a chocolate star to the top of the stable using the icing.

Read aloud **Luke 2:1–20**. Ask: why do you think God allowed Jesus to be born in a stable? If you could have chosen a place for Jesus to be born, where would you have chosen? What difference has Jesus' birth and life made for you?

FIRECRACKERS

Kids learn to shine brightly for Jesus.

WHAT YOU'LL NEED:

You'll need a Bible, kitchen-towel tubes, various colours of long metallic-paper strips, star stickers, glitter, glue, sugar paper and scissors.

FOR EXTRA IMPACT:

- Encourage the children to talk about good things they'll do during the week to honour God.

- Tape colourful metallic-paper strips to the end of a torch. Turn off the lights, and let the children shine the torch to create shimmering firework effects.

- Children can make colourful bookmarks by stapling metallic-paper strips to the end of a piece of card. Then write on the card, 'Let your light shine!'

WHAT TO DO

Decorate the kitchen-towel tube with stickers, glitter and sugar paper. Cut out a circle of sugar paper big enough to cover the bottom of the tube. Glue the circle to the tube, and glue long strips of metallic paper inside the tube so they dangle out the open end.

Read aloud **Matthew 5:16**. How is God's love like or unlike a firecracker? Once you've experienced God's love, what do you want to do with it? What are things we can do to shine brightly like fireworks with Jesus' love?

FLAME BOUQUETS

Kids make 'flame' bouquets for Pentecost Sunday.

WHAT YOU'LL NEED:

You'll need flame-coloured cellophane or tissue paper, gold foil, a ruler, scissors, florists' wire, crêpe-paper streamers, sugar paper and felt-tip pens.

FOR EXTRA IMPACT:

- Throw a party to celebrate that Pentecost is the birthday of the Church. Have cake, balloons, games and all the trimmings.

- Read aloud **Acts 2:1–4**, and ask the children to consider how the Holy Spirit helps us.

- Cut strawberries vertically to create wedge-shape slices. Let the children fill ice-cream cones with frozen yogurt and then press the strawberry 'flames' into the top of the yogurt for a 'fiery' treat.

See page 10.

WHAT TO DO

Cut flame-coloured cellophane or tissue paper and gold foil into 10 cm x 20 cm rectangles. Layer seven pieces on top of each other. Then fan out the pieces so all the colours show. Gather the rectangles 5 cm from the bottom. Wrap florists' wire and two 60 cm crêpe-paper streamers around the gathered end.

Let the children use sugar paper and felt-tip pens to make thank-you cards. Make one card to go along with each bouquet. The children can present them to church and children's leaders and helpers.

FLOWERPOT SCULPTURES

Kids can create beautiful, hand-picked flower gifts, perhaps for Mother's Day.

WHAT YOU'LL NEED:

You'll need small polystyrene cups, potting soil, assorted potted flowers and 30 cm pieces of kitchen foil.

FOR EXTRA IMPACT:

- Let older children paint small clay pots with non-toxic, shiny paints to use as planters.

- Get the children to stand in a circle and each grab hold of an edge of a lightweight blanket. Ask them to raise their hands, lifting the blanket overhead, and yell out some ways that God's love covers us.

- Read aloud **Psalm 52:8**, and discuss ways we can trust in God's unfailing love.

WHAT TO DO

Ask the children to think of the person they want to give a gift to and then choose a flower that reminds them of that person. They might choose a beautiful flower because their mum is beautiful or a tall flower because Aunt Jean is tall. Ask them to tell you why they chose their flowers.

Help the children transplant their flowers into the polystyrene cups, adding potting soil as needed. Place the cup in the centre of a piece of foil and press the foil around the cup's base and sides.

Say: God loves the person you're thinking of very much. His love covers us, like the foil covers the cup.

Encourage the children to sculpt creatively the foil to create a shimmering, delightful flowerpot that represents God's love for the flower recipient. Close in prayer, thanking God for the children and his love for everyone.

FOOTPRINTS IN THE SAND

Kids make imprints of their feet to remind them to walk with God.

WHAT YOU'LL NEED:

You'll need large sheets of black plastic, sand, plaster of Paris, water, a mixing bucket, a stirrer and metal eyelets. You'll also need a Bible.

FOR EXTRA IMPACT:

- Read aloud the poem 'Footprints in the Sand' by Mary Stevenson. You can find a copy online.

- Ask the children: how can we follow God and serve him?

- Ask: how does it feel to know God carries us during hard times? Close in prayer, thanking God for being with us always.

WHAT TO DO

Lay out sheets of black plastic. Pour sand 8 cm deep on to sections of the black plastic, one for each child. Mix enough water into the sand so it will hold a mould. Mix the plaster of Paris and water in the bucket according to the instructions.

Get each child to press one foot 5 cm into a sand section. Carefully pour plaster into each footprint. Then insert one metal eyelet in each print to hang it later. Clean out the eyelet opening if necessary. The plaster takes 30 minutes to harden.

While the prints are drying, read aloud from **Joshua 22:5**: 'Love the Lord your God, walk in all his ways, obey his commands, hold firmly to him, and serve him with all your heart and all your soul' (NLT). Ask: what does it mean to walk in God's ways?

Once the plaster has hardened, gently dig out the footprints and brush off the excess sand. The footprints should dry overnight before being hung on the wall.

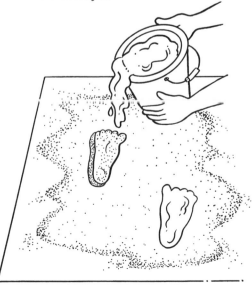

GARDEN-IN-A-POT

Kids celebrate God's gifts of nature with these colourful gardens.

WHAT YOU'LL NEED:

You'll need clay pots 10 cm in diameter, green floral foam, 10 cm plastic-foam balls cut in half, black pipe cleaners, cotton buds, googly eyes, PVA glue, extra-wide, extra-long jumbo craft sticks, 5 mm wooden dowels in 30 cm lengths, red, black and yellow non-toxic acrylic paint, paintbrushes and a hot-glue gun (adult use only).

FOR EXTRA IMPACT:

- Make butterflies by colouring coffee filter papers with pens and crayons. Pinch the filter in the middle, add a pipe cleaner folded in half for the antennae, and clip together with a clothes peg.

- Let the children fill in their gardens with artificial or tissue-paper flowers.

WHAT TO DO

Let the children make the following items for their gardens:

Pots—Paint a 10 cm clay pot. When the paint is dry, fill the pot with floral foam. Get an adult to use a hot-glue gun to tack the sides of the foam to the pot.

Ladybirds—Cover a foam-ball half with red paint. When the paint is dry, paint black dots using a cotton bud. Glue on two movable craft eyes. Push black pipe cleaners into the plastic foam for the legs and antennae. Push a wooden dowel into the flat side of the ladybird, and insert the dowel into the foam in the pot.

Sunflowers—Cover a foam-ball half with black paint. While the paint dries, paint ten craft sticks bright yellow. When the paint is dry, push the craft sticks around the outer edge of the foam ball to create the petals of the sunflower. Push a wooden dowel into the base of the rounded side of the sunflower (behind the petals), and insert the stick into the foam in the pot.

THE BIG BOOK OF BIBLE CRAFTS

GETHSEMANE SNACKS

Kids make this edible craft as a reminder of Jesus' time in Gethsemane.

WHAT YOU'LL NEED:

You'll need a Bible, digestive biscuits, jelly worm sweets, chocolate-covered raisins, Twiglets® or similar, small marshmallows, resealable food bags, paper plates, napkins and plastic spoons.

ALLERGY ALERT

See page 10.

FOR EXTRA IMPACT:

- As the children eat their snacks, ask: why did the disciples flee? How do you think Jesus felt when everyone left him?

- Read aloud **Mark 14:49**, and explain to the children what it means that the 'scriptures must be fulfilled'.

- Tell the children that **Isaiah 53** was written long before Jesus was born and foretold Jesus' death for our sins.

WHAT TO DO

Read aloud **Mark 14:32–50**. As you narrate the biblical account, ask volunteers to distribute paper plates, then pass out the snack ingredients that go with the story.

Give the children crumbled digestive biscuits and chocolate-covered raisins to represent the sandy ground and rocks where Jesus knelt. Children should pour the 'sand' on to the paper plate and scatter the 'rocks'.

Jelly worms represent the disciples' temptation to fall asleep. Marshmallows represent the soft places where the disciples rested their heads and slept. Twiglets® represent the swords and clubs carried by the men who came to arrest Jesus.

GIFT FOR MUM

Kids express their love to their mum or another special woman.

WHAT YOU'LL NEED:

You'll need a clear 35 mm film canister for each child (available from photo processors), 2.5 cm-wide ribbon or fabric strips, narrow ribbon, non-toxic fabric paints, wool, sequins or beads, tacky glue, scissors, paintbrushes, egg boxes, card, a ruler, pens and small wrapped sweets.

FOR EXTRA IMPACT:

- Read aloud **1 Corinthians 13:4**, and encourage the children to share ways their mums show them love.

- Ask the children to talk about ways they can show love to their mums. Encourage them to do at least one of those things during the week.

- Let the children each make a 'thank you' gift bag by writing words that describe their mum on the outside of a paper bag, placing the gift inside, and tying with colourful ribbon.

WHAT TO DO

Work with the open end of the canister up. Glue the wide ribbon or fabric strip around the bottom half of the film canister. Then glue narrow ribbon along the top edge of the wide ribbon.

Remove the canister's cap and set it aside. Paint a face on the canister with fabric paint. Cut and unravel wool pieces and glue them around the back and sides of the canister for hair. Add sequins or beads for earrings.

Cut and paint an egg-box section to make a hat. When the paint is dry, bend up a brim around the edge. Add ribbons or sequins for decoration.

Cut an 8 cm-diameter circle from card. Write 'God fills mums with LOVE!' around the outside edge of the circle. Glue the film canister to the middle of the circle. Take off the hat and fill the canister with small sweets. Put the cap and then the hat back on. Then give it to Mum!

ALLERGY ALERT

See page 10.

GOD'S BLOSSOMS

Kids learn they can trust God to take care of all their needs.

WHAT YOU'LL NEED:

You'll need a Bible, eggshell halves, non-toxic acrylic paints, paintbrushes, green pipe cleaners and a hot-glue gun (adult use only). (As an alternative to eggshells, you could use egg-box sections.)

FOR EXTRA IMPACT:

- Let the children cut out and tape tissue-paper leaves on to their flower stems.

- Use the inside of the eggs to make scrambled eggs. As you eat the scrambled eggs, share ways God takes care of us.

WHAT TO DO

Before the children arrive, carefully crack the eggs so you have two intact eggshell halves. Wash the shells, and let them dry. Poke a small hole in the bottom of each shell.

Give each child an eggshell half to paint any colour they want with acrylic paint. Allow the shells to dry. Then insert a green pipe cleaner through the hole. It can be twisted to create leaves. Then get an adult to hot-glue the tip inside the egg.

Read aloud **Matthew 6:25–34**. Discuss with the children how we don't need to worry about our lives because God is always taking care of us. Tell them that whenever they see flowers, they can remember that God is taking care of them, even as he takes care of the 'little' things.

ALLERGY ALERT

See page 10.

GRASS SEED SAMSON

Kids can sow grass seed, then wait for Samson's 'hair' to grow.

WHAT YOU'LL NEED:

You'll need 1 rinsed carton for each child (such as a 200 ml juice carton), scissors, potting soil, grass seed, sugar paper, felt-tip pens and glue sticks.

FOR EXTRA IMPACT:

- Explain how God gave Samson a special gift of strength, but Delilah stole his strength. Read aloud **Judges 16:15–19**.

- Ask: what are some special gifts God has given you?

- Let the children make a Samson snack by icing a biscuit, then decorating it with dried fruit or sweets for the face and liquorice or strawberry laces for Samson's hair.

ALLERGY ALERT
See page 10.

WHAT TO DO

Cut off the top of the carton so the carton becomes an open container. Glue sugar paper around the carton, then draw a Samson face (up to the forehead) on the sugar paper. The top of the carton is the hairline.

Fill each carton with potting soil to about 1.5 cm from the top. Then sprinkle grass seed on the soil, and cover the seed with a thin layer of soil.

Set the 'Samsons' on a sunny windowsill and keep them well watered. After a few days, each Samson's hair will begin to grow! When it gets long enough, the children can cut the hair.

HANDCRAFTED FLOWERS

Kids love making these edible flowers.

WHAT YOU'LL NEED:

You'll need fruit pastilles, rolling pins, sugar, baking paper, scissors and plastic food bags.

ALLERGY ALERT

See page 10.

FOR EXTRA IMPACT:

- Read aloud **1 Peter 1:24–25**. Ask the children what they think the passage means.

- Let the children eat their flower petals one at a time and compare how that is like or unlike what happens when flowers wither and fall away.

- Get the children to write, '"The word of the Lord endures for ever"—1 Peter 1:25' on a strip of card. They can use the strips as bookmarks to remind them of the strength of God's word.

WHAT TO DO

Cut the fruit pastilles in half and use the halves to design a flower on a sugared piece of baking paper. Use one sliced fruit pastille for the centre and halves of different colours for the petals. Use green fruit pastilles to form the stems and leaves.

When the design is finished, sprinkle sugar on the fruit pastilles to keep them from sticking. Roll out the flowers, then carefully slide them into plastic food bags.

HEART MARKS

Kids make these decorative bookmarks as a perfect gift for housebound church members.

WHAT YOU'LL NEED:

You'll need 4 cm x 13 cm craft-foam strips and craft-foam scraps of various colours. You'll also need scissors, glue, a hole punch, a ruler, multicoloured wool and permanent fine-tipped markers.

FOR EXTRA IMPACT:

• Ask the children to write, '"Give thanks to the God of gods. His love endures for ever"—Psalm 136:2' on the back of their bookmarks.

• Close in prayer, and encourage each child to give thanks to God for one thing.

WHAT TO DO

Give each child a 4 cm x 13 cm craft-foam strip. Ask them to cut ten hearts of various sizes from the craft-foam scraps. The hearts can be of any colour and must be small enough to fit on the foam strip.

Let the children arrange and then glue the hearts to the craft-foam strips. Then punch a single hole at the top centre of the bookmark.

To finish the bookmarks, cut six 25 cm lengths of the multicoloured wool. Hold the wool pieces with the ends even. Fold the wool pieces in half, and push the fold through the hole at the top centre of the bookmark to create a 2.5 cm loop. Pull the wool ends through the loop and gently pull to make a snug knot.

HUMAN BEANS

Kids can use this outreach craft as a great way to send a loving message to friends and neighbours.

WHAT YOU'LL NEED:

You'll need a 40 cm section of nylon tights, including the foot, for each child. You'll also need dried beans, googly eyes, glue, craft foam, pom-poms, scissors, card, a ruler, curling ribbon, a hole punch and glitter pens.

FOR EXTRA IMPACT:

- Read aloud **Psalm 52:8,** and discuss ways we can trust in God's unfailing love.

- Ask: how is reaching out to others like or unlike a tree flourishing in God's love?

- Ask older children to write, '"I trust in God's unfailing love for ever and ever"—Psalm 52:8b' on the back of the human bean cards.

WHAT TO DO

Fill the foot of the tights with dried beans until the section is about two-thirds full, then tie a knot around the open end of the tights. (Make sure children don't eat the beans!) Cut the remainder of the tights in thin strips to make hair or fold over the top of the knot for a hat.

Cut out two feet from craft foam, then glue them to the bottom of the 'human bean'. Allow the glue to dry. Decorate the human beans with googly eyes and pom-pom noses.

Fold an 8 cm x 13 cm piece of card in half and cut out a bean-shaped card. Write 'From one human bean to another—God loves you!' in glitter pen on the cards. Punch a hole in the cards, and use curling ribbon to attach them to the human beans. The children can give their human beans to friends and family.

FROM ONE HUMAN BEAN TO ANOTHER- GOD LOVES YOU!

LEAFY T-SHIRTS

Kids learn about God's creation.

WHAT YOU'LL NEED:

You'll need a Bible, news-paper, non-toxic fabric paints, paintbrushes, a container of water, a prewashed plain T-shirt for each child, small craft sponges, fresh, green leaves and painting shirts. You'll need to press the green leaves between layers of newspaper for one week prior to use.

FOR EXTRA IMPACT:

• Take the children on a nature walk to collect leaves, pine cones and other natural items for a display in your meet-ing space. While walking, talk about God's creation.

• Make a classroom banner by letting the children stamp the leaves on to muslin or cotton fabric. Use a fabric pen to write the words of **Revelation 4:11** on the banner. Attach ribbon to the top as a hanger.

• Make environmentally friendly greetings cards by stamping paint-coated leaves on to recycled paper.

WHAT TO DO

Cover the work area with newspaper. Fold newspaper inside the body and sleeves of the T-shirts. Then lay the shirts on the table, and smooth out any wrinkles.

Wet a paintbrush and squeeze most of the water out of it. Use the brush to coat a sponge with one colour of paint. Carefully dab the sponge on the veined side of the leaf, including the stem. Turn the leaf over and gently press it on to the T-shirt. (Tell the children to press, but not to rub the leaves.) Pick the leaf up by the stem and check the print. Add more or less paint next time as needed. Leave the newspaper inside the shirt until it's dry.

Read aloud **Revelation 4:11**. What does this verse teach us about how we should respond to God when we look at creation?

LET IT SHINE

Kids learn to light the path to faith in Christ at Halloween.

WHAT YOU'LL NEED:

You'll need paper bags, cookie cutters, pencils, LED battery-operated tea lights and Blu-tack® or similar.

FOR EXTRA IMPACT:

- Read aloud **Psalm 119:105**. Encourage the children to share ways God's word can light their path.

- Read aloud **Matthew 5:14–16**. Challenge the children to think of a good deed that can be a light to others during the week.

- Discuss other ways we can be God's light for the world at Halloween.

WHAT TO DO

Distribute the paper bags, and get the children to draw round cookie cutters to make hearts, crosses or other shapes on the bags. Then use pencils to poke holes through the bags about 1 cm apart around the traced shapes. (Putting Blu-tack® inside the bag at the point where you want to make the hole can help.)

Sit in a circle and dim the lights. Pass round some LED battery-operated tea lights (not real tea lights!) so the children can take turns at seeing the light shining through their bag.

Close in prayer, asking God to help people who live in darkness see the light of Christ and trust him as their Saviour.

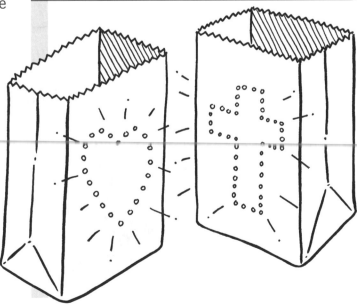

LITTLE LAMB CARDS

Kids make little lambs to celebrate the Lamb of God.

WHAT YOU'LL NEED:

You'll need a sheet of card around 22 cm x 28 cm, folded in half, a small jingle bell and a white pipe cleaner for each lamb. You'll also need non-toxic ink stamp pads, black felt-tip pens, pencils, cotton wool balls, glue, scissors and wipes for cleaning ink off fingers.

FOR EXTRA IMPACT:

• Read aloud **John 1:29**. Ask older children to write the verse inside their cards.

• Ask: what does it mean that Jesus takes away the sin of the world?

• Close in prayer, thanking God for sending Jesus, the Lamb of God, to die for our sins.

WHAT TO DO

Ask the children to press a fingertip on to the stamp pad and then on to the left of the card front's centre. The fingerprint is the lamb's head. Pencil in an oval to outline the lamb's body. Let the children glue cotton-wool balls inside the outline and then draw ears, eyes, nose and feet with a felt-tip pen.

Attach a bell by inserting a pipe cleaner through the bell's loop and punching the wire ends through the card at the lamb's neck. Twist the wire ends to secure the bell, and trim away the excess wire. Get the children to write their names inside their cards.

MACARONI NAME TAGS

Kids learn about the meaning of names.

WHAT YOU'LL NEED:

For the name tags, you'll need badge-sized pieces of card, glue, uncooked alphabet macaroni, felt-tip pens and badge pins. You'll also need a names book and a Bible.

FOR EXTRA IMPACT:

- Use a hairdryer to speed up the drying time of the name tags. Let older children dry their own name tags.

- Let children write their name and its meaning on sugar paper. Have felt-tip pens, ribbons and other collage materials on hand to decorate.

- Ask children to draw a picture of each family member and write the person's full name and its meanings on the paper. Draw a title page, and write 'My Family Names Book' on it. Then put the pictures together and staple them to form a book.

WHAT TO DO

Give each child a badge-sized piece of card. Let the children use the alphabet macaroni to spell their names and then use different colour felt-tip pens to decorate the macaroni.

Ask the children to glue their name to the card and then stick the back of a badge pin to the back of the card. Let it dry.

Read aloud **Matthew 16:17–18**. Say: Jesus changed Simon's name to *Peter*, which means 'rock'. How many of you know what your name means? Use a names book to find the meaning of children's names. Say: Jesus helped Peter be a strong rock for the church. Would you like God to help the meaning of your name be true? (Use tact where a child has a name with a negative meaning.)

FRONT

BACK

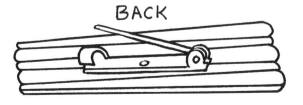

MEMORABLE MONTAGE

Kids create place mats to celebrate thankfulness.

WHAT YOU'LL NEED:

You'll need 30 cm x 45 cm sheets of sugar paper, magazines with suitable pictures, scissors, glue and self-adhesive covering film. Ask the children to bring in copies of their favourite photos.

FOR EXTRA IMPACT:

• Ask the children to turn to a partner and share a memory of an event they're thankful for.

• Let the children make place mats for family members to use as a discussion starter about thankfulness.

• Read aloud **Acts 27:35**, and ask: why is it important for us to give thanks to God?

WHAT TO DO

Encourage the children to cut and arrange their photos to make a collage on one side of their sugar paper. If they don't have photos, give them magazines and let them cut out pictures of things they're thankful for.

Glue the photos and pictures to the paper and allow to dry. To protect the place mat, carefully cover both sides with self-adhesive covering film.

Let the children each choose one photo or picture from their place mat and share why they're thankful for what it shows. Close with a prayer thanking God for all the wonderful things he gives us.

MINI EASTER GARDEN

Kids learn about the garden tomb that was empty on Easter morning.

WHAT YOU'LL NEED:

You'll need planting soil, moss or cut grass or sand, craft sticks, glue, small pots, flat stones large enough to cover the pots, egg-box cups (or other small containers), small flowers and gravel. You'll also need a shallow dish or tray for each child.

FOR EXTRA IMPACT:

- Read aloud **Luke 24:5–8**, and ask the children why they think the women were afraid. Ask: how do you think you would have felt?

- Ask: how do you think the women felt when they realised Jesus had risen from the dead? How does that make you feel today?

- Give each child a hollow chocolate Easter egg as a reminder to celebrate the empty tomb.

ALLERGY ALERT

See page 10.

WHAT TO DO

Fill a tray with soil and arrange the soil to make a hill on one side of the tray and a flat area on the other. Cover the soil with moss, grass or sand.

Make crosses by glueing craft sticks together. Then place them on the hilltop. Press the small pot into the 'hillside' to make a cave or tomb. Place the stone over the mouth of the tomb.

Press the egg-box cups into the soil around the flat 'garden' area and fill them with the small flowers. Use gravel to make a path to the tomb to show how the disciples ran there on Easter morning.

When the scenes are completed, gather children around the gardens and retell the Easter story. As you tell about the rock being rolled away, have children move the stones from their 'tombs' to show that they're empty.

MUSICAL INSTRUMENTS

Kids create a joyful noise with these musical instruments.

WHAT YOU'LL NEED:

You'll need paper plates, beer-bottle tops or wine-bottle screw caps or similar, strong thread, a ruler, large beads, wooden dowels, a hole punch, scissors, staplers, jar lids, sticky tape and 7 mm elastic. In advance, carefully pierce 2 holes in each jar lid and 1 in each bottle top or cap (this can be tricky; you can use jingle bells as an alternative). Discard any bottle tops that have sharp points where the hole was pierced.

FOR EXTRA IMPACT:

- Read aloud **Psalm 98:4–6**, and ask: how does God feel when we praise him? How does it feel to praise God?

- Put on praise music and let the children play along with their instruments.

WHAT TO DO

Twirling drums—Staple two facing paper plates together around the edges. Punch two holes along the edges on opposite sides of the plates. Get the children to tie a large bead to a 20 cm section of heavy-duty thread, and tie the other end through one hole on each plate. Repeat this for the second hole. Tape a wooden dowel on the centre edge of the plates below the two holes. Once the dowel is attached, children can roll the dowel between their hands to twirl the drum and create a unique beat.

Tambourines—Staple two facing paper plates together around the edges. Use a hole punch to make eight holes around the edges of the plates (or fewer if you have fewer bottle tops or caps). Ask the children to string two bottle tops on to 7 cm pieces of heavy-duty thread. Tie the thread through the holes in the plates. Keep the bottle tops on the same side of the plate. Alternatively, string jingle bells to each plate.

Castanets—Each child will need four jar lids to make a set of castanets. Help the children tie 7 cm sections of 7 mm elastic through the holes in the jar lids and cut off any extra. Children will wear one castanet on each thumb and the other on their forefingers or middle fingers.

PRAYER GARDENS

Kids learn how prayer causes wonderful things to grow.

WHAT YOU'LL NEED:

You'll need an egg box for each child, felt-tip pens, stickers, rubber bands, potting soil and flower seeds.

FOR EXTRA IMPACT:

- Read aloud **Psalm 17:6**, and encourage the children to share different ways we can call on God to hear our prayers.

- Ask children to share 'praise reports' of ways God has answered their prayers.

- Ask older children to write out Psalm 17:6. Encourage them to read the scripture each day before saying their prayer-garden prayers.

WHAT TO DO

Give each child an egg box. Get them to use felt-tip pens and stickers to create a garden scene inside the top of the box. Fill each egg cup with soil and a flower seed. Secure the lids with rubber bands so the children can safely take the boxes home.

Ask the children to think of someone who is in need. Encourage them to pray daily for that person and then add a quarter of a teaspoon of water to each egg cup. Say: when we pray for people, God causes wonderful things to grow in their lives.

Send a note home telling parents to transplant the seedlings soon after shoots appear.

PRAYER WHEEL

Kids create a fun way to bring the habit of prayer to their family table.

WHAT YOU'LL NEED:

You'll need a Bible, card, a ruler, felt-tip pens, scissors, paper fasteners, glue, craft items for decorating, paintbrushes, paint, painting shirts, a table cover and a hairdryer.

FOR EXTRA IMPACT:

- Encourage the children to share ways they've seen God answer prayers.

- Reinforce the habit of mealtime prayers by asking the children to say a blessing before each snack.

- Make a prayer wheel for the group with each child's name in one of the pie sections. Use the wheel to kick off prayer time before each group begins.

WHAT TO DO

Find out from the children if any of them say mealtime prayers at home and if so, ask them to choose three favourite things their family or someone else's family prays for. Number these 1, 2 and 3, and list them on three edges of a 13 cm x 13 cm square of card. Draw a pie chart on the card, and divide the chart to make a section for each family member. Write a family member's name in each piece.

Cut out an arrow from card. Make a spinner by pushing a paper fastener through the end of the card arrow and into the centre of the pie chart. Let the children decorate their prayer wheels. A hairdryer can be used to dry any paint.

Read aloud **Acts 27:35**. Ask: why does God want us to pray to him? How often does your family pray together?

Say: use this prayer wheel at mealtimes to help your family to pray. Spin the arrow, and the person whose name it lands on says the prayer that night. If that person can't think of anything to pray for, ask him or her to choose one of the numbered items on the wheel.

PULLED PALMS

Kids make palm branches to celebrate Jesus.

WHAT YOU'LL NEED:

You'll need scissors, glue and 8 sheets of paper for each palm branch.

FOR EXTRA IMPACT:

- Read aloud **Mark 11:1–10**, and discuss how Jesus would arrive into town today.

- Choose a child to play Jesus, and ask him or her to parade around your room while the other children wave their palm branches.

- Lead the children in singing their favourite praise song as they wave their palms to the music.

WHAT TO DO

To make a palm branch, roll the first sheet of paper lengthwise into a tube 1.5 cm in diameter. When halfway rolled, lay another sheet of paper on top of the unrolled portion. Continue rolling until the second sheet is rolled halfway. Add additional pieces of paper in the same manner. Glue the last edge in place.

Then cut slits approximately 5 cm long and 0.5 cm wide around one end of the tube. Gently pull the paper from the centre of the roll. Twist the roll slightly as you pull. Brush the paper fringes to make them stand out.

Now you're ready for a Palm Sunday procession. Let the children wave their palms as you lead them in this rhyming cheer:

Who do we want? Jesus!
Why do we want him? He's our King!
How do we praise him? With our palms!
When do we praise him? When we sing!

RAINBOW LIGHT CATCHER

Kids learn to cooperate with this colourful craft.

WHAT YOU'LL NEED:

You'll need a Bible, clear self-adhesive covering film, scissors, a permanent marker pen, masking tape, several sheets of red, orange, yellow, green, blue, indigo and violet tissue paper, a ruler, cotton-wool balls, a hole punch and string.

FOR EXTRA IMPACT:

- Share with the children some promises we have from God.

- Let them talk about the people who are most trustworthy in their lives and why they can be trusted.

- Let them make a miniature version of the rainbow to take home and hang in their rooms as a reminder of their promise to cooperate with others.

WHAT TO DO

Before the children arrive, unwind and cut off a 1.5 m section of self-adhesive covering film, with the backing still on it, on a long table. Lay the film lengthwise with the clear side up. Draw the seven divisions of a rainbow across it with a permanent marker. Turn the film over and remove the backing so the sticky side is up. Hold it down at each end with masking tape.

Get the children to cut tissue paper into 5 cm squares and place the squares in same-colour piles. Pinch the centre of each square so the sides of the tissue paper 'fan out'. Stick the pinched part of each tissue-paper square to the covering film. Fill each section of the rainbow with many pieces of tissue paper. The colours should be in this order: red, orange, yellow, green, indigo, blue and violet.

Fill the remaining areas of the covering film with cotton-wool balls to make clouds. Using the hole punch, make holes 10 cm from the top, and string up the rainbow in an open area so light can show through it.

Read aloud **Genesis 9:12–17**. Explain that a covenant is an agreement between two people. Say: God made a promise to us. Let's promise to work harder at cooperating with one another.

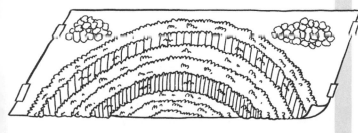

RIBBON PRAYER

This craft is designed to help children learn the Lord's Prayer.

WHAT YOU'LL NEED:

You'll need 10 cm each of blue, white, purple, green, yellow, red and gold ribbon for each child, and 10 cm of rough twine. You'll also need a Bible.

FOR EXTRA IMPACT:

- Let the children choose a favourite song and dance along to the music, waving their prayer ribbons.

- Cut 30 cm sugar-paper strips for each different ribbon colour. Tape the strips to the end of a kitchen-towel tube to make prayer tubes.

- Let the children make extra prayer ribbons to give to friends or family to teach others about the Lord's Prayer.

WHAT TO DO

Read aloud **Matthew 6:9–13**.

Say: blue can be a colour for fathers. Say, 'Our Father in heaven' as you hold the blue ribbon.

White can represent holiness. Say, 'Hallowed be your name' as you tie the white ribbon to the blue one.

Purple is a majestic colour. Say, 'Your kingdom come, your will be done' as you tie purple to white.

Green is one of the colours of the earth. Say, 'On earth as it is in heaven' as you tie green to purple.

Yellow reminds us of wheat. Say, 'Give us today our daily bread' as you tie yellow to green.

Red reminds us of Jesus' blood. By trusting in Jesus, we're forgiven. Say, 'And forgive us our debts, as we also have forgiven our debtors' as you tie red to yellow.

The rough twine represents evil. Say, 'And lead us not into temptation, but deliver us from evil' as you tie the twine to the red ribbon.

And gold reminds us of God's heavenly kingdom. Say, 'For yours is the kingdom, the power and the glory forever. Amen' as you tie gold to the twine.

SAILING BOATS

Kids learn to trust God in the storms of life.

WHAT YOU'LL NEED:

For each sailing boat, you'll need glue, sticky tape, ½ a plastic-foam sandwich box, a larger plastic-foam food tray, an empty thread spool and a thin straw. You'll also need sails and flags cut from card, a small paddling pool filled with water (carefully supervised at all times!) and a Bible.

FOR EXTRA IMPACT:

- Share with the children a time in your life when God was trustworthy during a storm.

- Ask the children to form groups, and give each group a large cardboard box to colour to resemble a boat. Let them act out Paul's voyage.

- Make sailing-boat snacks. Press carrot sticks into peeled hard-boiled egg halves. Cut pre-packed cheese slices on the diagonal, and carefully press the triangles around cocktail sticks to make the sails.

ALLERGY ALERT

See page 10.

WHAT TO DO

Glue the half of a sandwich box upside down on the upper side of the food tray to make the ship and its cabin. Next, glue the spool to the top of the sandwich box. Put the straw through the hole in the spool and punch it into the top of the sandwich box (but not through the food tray). Glue or tape sails and flags to the straw 'mast'.

Let the children test the seaworthiness of their boats in the paddling pool. Then tell them the story of Paul's voyage in **Acts 27**. Ask: how do you think Paul and the sailors felt during the storm? How did God take care of the people on the ship? What are some 'storms' or hard things that threaten to shipwreck our lives? How can we trust God to take care of us during those storms?

THE BIG BOOK OF BIBLE CRAFTS

SANDCASTLE CLAY

Kids learn about God's hidden treasures.

WHAT YOU'LL NEED:

You'll need a large bucket, a large stick, clean fine-grain play sand, a scoop, PVA glue (a large quantity), plastic plates or plastic food trays and painting aprons.

FOR EXTRA IMPACT:

- Read aloud **Deuteronomy 33:19**, and ask the children how their sandcastle creations are like or unlike treasures in the sand.

- Hide little plastic toys in a paddling pool filled with sand. Let the children take turns finding the 'treasures' hidden in the sand and then returning them for others to find.

WHAT TO DO

Make sure the children wear aprons for this craft. Pour the sand into the bucket. Then pour glue on to the sand, and stir with a large stick until all the sand is moistened. Give each of the children a plastic plate (or plastic food tray). The children can use the sand to make small sandcastles or other sculptures on the plastic plates. Air-dry the finished creations.

SAND SCULPTURES

Kids will appreciate the details God put into each of us as they create these unique paperweights.

WHAT YOU'LL NEED:

You'll need a Bible, a large bucket, a large stick, clean play sand, a scoop, PVA glue (a large quantity), poster paints, assorted beads, plastic lids, cocktail sticks (watch younger children carefully) and painting aprons.

FOR EXTRA IMPACT:

- Read aloud **Psalm 139:14**, and ask: what do you think it means to be fearfully and wonderfully made?

- Ask: how does it feel to know that God created each one of us with special gifts?

- Ask the children to draw a self-portrait and write on it, 'I am fearfully and wonderfully made.' Then ask them to find a partner, show each other their pictures, and talk about the special gifts God has given them.

WHAT TO DO

Read aloud **Psalm 139:13–16**. Say: imagine how God worked to create the earth, and imagine how he worked on each of you.

Ask the children to put on painting aprons. Pour the sand into the bucket. Ask the children to reach into the bucket and lift out a handful of sand. Tell them to let the sand trickle through their fingers. Say: God created every grain of sand, just as he created every one of us.

Pour glue into the sand bucket, and stir with a large stick until all the sand is moistened. Ask the children to choose a plastic lid to be a base for their paperweight. Scoop the sand mixture into children's hands, and let them form paperweights. They can decorate their paperweights by pressing beads into the sand or dropping paint on to the sand and swirling it with a cocktail stick. They can press their fingers or cocktail sticks into the sand mixture to make different shapes and textures.

Let the paperweights dry for one week, then peel away the plastic base.

SCRATCHBOARD PICTURES

Kids learn that Jesus helps us see what's hidden.

WHAT YOU'LL NEED:

You'll need a Bible, heavy paper, crayons, black poster paint in small dishes, cocktail sticks (watch younger children carefully), washing-up liquid and paintbrushes.

FOR EXTRA IMPACT:

- Have several hairdryers on hand, and let the older children blow-dry their paintings to speed up drying time.

- Ask the children to close their eyes while one child turns a torch off or on and hides it under a bowl. Then get the children to guess whether the light is on or off.

- Play a game of Hide the Object with the children having to listen to the leader's clues to find the hidden object. Let the child who finds the object hide it for the next round.

WHAT TO DO

Mix a drop of washing up-liquid into each small dish of black paint. Get the children to colour their entire paper with crayon, telling them to make a thick layer of crayon as they colour. Then get them to paint black all over the layer of crayon. Let the paint dry. Scratch a picture into the black painted surface with a cocktail stick. The beautiful colours underneath will show through!

Read aloud **Mark 4:21–23**. Ask: what do you think Jesus meant by 'whatever is hidden'? How will Jesus help us see what's hidden? How was our black picture like or unlike not knowing everything Jesus wants us to know? How is our scratched picture like or unlike knowing everything Jesus wants us to know? How can we be better listeners to learn from Jesus?

SILLYETTES

Kids love making these fun self-portraits.

WHAT YOU'LL NEED:

You'll need sheets of A3 paper, masking tape, an overhead projector, marker pens, glue and craft materials, such as feathers, fabric, paper, beads, wool or glitter.

FOR EXTRA IMPACT:

- Read aloud **Psalm 139:14** and ask the children: in what ways are God's works wonderful? How is that like the way God created us?

- Ask: why do you think God made each one of us with different characteristics and gifts?

- Ask the children to talk about one of their favourite characteristics or gifts. Close in prayer, thanking God that each of us is wonderfully made.

WHAT TO DO

Tape a sheet of paper to the wall. Place an overhead projector on the other side of the room. Ask a child to stand between the projector and the paper so that his or her silhouette fills the paper. Use a marker pen to draw around the child's silhouette.

Write the child's name on the back of the paper, and give the child the silhouette. The children can use craft materials to make their silhouettes into 'sillyettes'. When they have finished, hang the portraits in your meeting space.

SNOW ANGELS

Kids love making these fun angels.

ALL AGES

WHAT YOU'LL NEED:

You'll need a long roll of paper, cut into sheets large enough for a child to lie on, thick felt-tip pens, paintbrushes, paint and painting aprons.

FOR EXTRA IMPACT:

- Give the children craft supplies, such as wool, sequins, googly eyes, ribbons and lace, to use as they decorate their angels.

- Read aloud **Hebrews 13:2**, and ask: do you believe angels help us today? Have you ever had an encounter with an angel?

- Discuss how we can be 'angels' to others through acts of kindness.

WHAT TO DO

Children can create snow angels on large sheets of paper. Ask a child to lie on the paper, legs slightly apart. A volunteer then draws the child's outline, but not the arms or insides of the legs. Give the child two felt-tip pens of the same colour—one to hold in each hand—and get them to move their arms up and down so that they draw long arcs on the paper. Connect the leg outlines with a curve to represent the bottom of an angel's robe. Then get the children to decorate their life-size angels with felt-tip pens or paint.

SPOON PUPPETS

Kids love making these fun storytelling props.

WHAT YOU'LL NEED:

You'll need a wooden spoon for each child, glue, foil, felt-tip pens, cotton-wool balls, wool, fake fur, fabric, ribbon and scissors.

FOR EXTRA IMPACT:

- Ask the children to form groups, and let each group select a Bible story, such as that of Shadrach, Meshach and Abednego (see Daniel 3). Then each child can make one of the story characters, and the group can put on a puppet show for the others.

- Give the children large plastic disposable spoons, and let each child make several different Bible characters.

- Have shoeboxes, egg boxes and other craft supplies on hand so the children can make play sets for their puppets.

WHAT TO DO

Give each child a wooden spoon.

Ask the children to choose a person from the Bible and draw that person's face on the oval part of the spoon. They can then dress the person according to what he or she would have worn.

Cotton-wool balls or wool can be used for beards or hair. Fake fur and fabric are good for clothing, and foil makes great weapons and armour.

Once the spoon puppets are made, encourage the children to use them to retell Bible stories.

SPRAY ART

Kids create colourful paintings.

WHAT YOU'LL NEED:

You'll need pump spray bottles, water, food colouring, a 6 m piece of rope, clothes pegs, large sheets of paper and painting shirts.

FOR EXTRA IMPACT:

- Read aloud **Genesis 37:3**, and ask the children to describe what they think Joseph's colourful coat looked like.

- Help the children cut a 'robe' from a roll of paper. Let them cut their paintings into squares and glue the squares on to their robes to make colourful coats.

- Get the children to spray-paint coffee filter papers and hang them from the ceiling when dry to create a colourful scene.

WHAT TO DO

Before the children arrive, fill spray bottles with water and drops of food colouring. Shake well to mix. Tie a 6 m piece of rope about 1.2 m from the ground between two trees or poles outside. Peg sheets of paper to the rope.

Make sure the children wear painting shirts. Let them choose a spray bottle to spray near the top of their paper. Then let them use spray bottles with other colours to spray the rest of their paper. The coloured water will drip and run. Colours will mix, creating beautiful paintings.

Once a child has finished his or her painting, remove it and allow to dry on the grass. Place another sheet of paper in its place, and allow another child to create a masterpiece.

STAINED-GLASS CRAFT

Kids make colourful
stained-glass art.

WHAT YOU'LL NEED:

You'll need coloured tissue
paper, clear self-adhesive
covering film, a ruler and
scissors.

FOR EXTRA IMPACT:

- Let the children use PVA glue
  to stick different colour tissue
  paper squares on the outside
  of clean glass jars. When dry,
  add tea light candles to the
  stained-glass candle holders.

- Make stained-glass cookies.
  Cut shapes from chilled
  cookie dough. Cut smaller
  shapes inside the cookies, fill
  with crushed boiled sweets
  and bake.

ALLERGY ALERT

See page 10

WHAT TO DO

Give each child two 25 cm x 25 cm pieces
of clear self-adhesive covering film. Peel
the backing off the first piece and lay it
down tacky side up.

Let the children tear small pieces of tissue
paper and place them on the tacky side
of the self-adhesive film in the shape of a
cross, fish, heart or crown. When finished,
peel the backing off the second piece of
self-adhesive film and carefully lay it over
the artwork with the tacky side down.

Cut around the shape with scissors. The
children can lightly moisten one side and
stick their stained-glass art to a window.

SUMMER FUN T-SHIRTS

Kids make colourful T-shirts as fun summer-memory keepsakes.

WHAT YOU'LL NEED:

You'll need a white, 100% cotton T-shirt for each child, white glue, non-toxic cold-water dye, water, spray bottles, thick-bristle paintbrushes, newspaper, painting shirts and optional latex gloves (check for allergies).

FOR EXTRA IMPACT:

- Let the children model their T-shirts (when the dye has been set) and talk about their summer memories.

- Read aloud **Ecclesiastes 3:1** and say: summer is over, and we are entering a new season of school. Ask: what's the most exciting thing about starting a new school year?

- Ask children to share any fears they have about the upcoming school year and pray for those concerns.

WHAT TO DO

Before the children arrive, mix the dye colours according to the package instructions, and fill the spray bottles with different colours.

Place several layers of newspaper inside the T-shirts. Get the children to put on painting shirts and then use glue to 'paint' on their T-shirts a basic drawing that symbolises their favourite thing about summer. Allow the glue to dry on the front, then decorate the back.

Once the glue has dried completely, take the shirts outside. Get the children to spray their entire T-shirts on the front and back with the dye. (You may want them to wear latex gloves.) Allow the shirts to dry overnight, and wash the shirts according to the dye instructions to set the dye.

SWEET ANGELS

Kids make edible angel treats.

WHAT YOU'LL NEED:

You'll need chilled cookie dough, a knife (adult use only), plastic knives, baking trays, an oven, a spatula, cooling racks, oven gloves and baking paper.

ALLERGY ALERT
See page 10.

FOR EXTRA IMPACT:

- Let the children decorate the cooled cookies with icing and cake decorations such as sprinkles.

- Read aloud **Luke 1:8–19** as the children eat their angels.

- Children can make angel-cookie ornaments and decorate an 'angel tree' for Christmas.

WHAT TO DO

Ask the children to wash their hands. Cut a thin circle of chilled cookie dough for each child. Help each child to cut a triangle with a rounded bottom out of their dough circle, for the angel's body. Use the two remaining semicircles to create wings. To create the angel's head, give each child a pinch of dough to roll into a ball and flatten.

Ask the children to arrange their dough in angel formations on baking trays lined with baking paper, and bake according to the pack instructions.

SWEET SHEEP

Kids love making and eating these cute sheep.

WHAT YOU'LL NEED:

You'll need chocolate muffins, icing, desiccated coconut, raisins, chocolate fingers or chocolate mint sticks, plastic knives and paper plates.

ALLERGY ALERT

See page 10.

FOR EXTRA IMPACT:

- Ask the children to set their sheep on a table and talk about how each one is different. Ask: how is that like or unlike how we are all different?

- Read aloud **Psalm 100:3**. Ask: what does it mean that we are the sheep of God's pasture?

- Ask: how do you feel knowing that you belong to God?

WHAT TO DO

Ask the children to wash their hands, then get them to peel the muffin papers off the muffins and place the muffins upside down on paper plates. Ice the muffins, leaving the sheep's 'face' plain. Sprinkle a layer of desiccated coconut over the icing for wool.

Stick a raisin into the icing on either side of the sheep's head to represent ears. Use half a chocolate finger or half a chocolate mint stick for each leg. You can create eyes from the icing.

Let the children enjoy eating their Sweet Sheep.

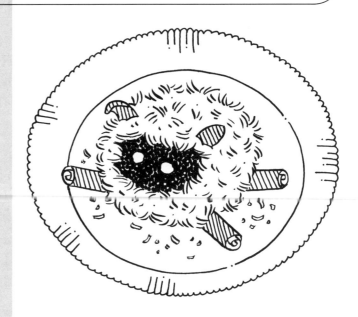

THANKFUL TURKEYS

Kids make these tasty 'turkey' treats to remind them to give thanks to God every day.

WHAT YOU'LL NEED:

For each 'turkey', you'll need a red apple, cocktail sticks (watch younger children carefully), small sweets such as dolly mixture, red liquorice, larger yellow sweets such as Haribo®, a large marshmallow and black gel icing. You'll also need card, felt-tip pens and scissors.

ALLERGY ALERT

See page 10.

FOR EXTRA IMPACT:

- Read aloud **Psalm 118:28–29**, and ask: why should we give thanks to God?

- Ask the children to talk about things they're thankful for while eating the Thankful Turkeys.

- Close in prayer and encourage the children to each give thanks to God for one thing.

WHAT TO DO

Set the apple on a work surface. Stick four cocktail sticks in a semicircle into the top of the apple. Spear four small sweets (such as dolly mixture) on each of the cocktail sticks to create multicoloured tail feathers (younger children will need help with the cocktail sticks).

For the turkey's head, stick a cocktail stick into the top of the apple opposite the tail feathers. Cut a 2 cm section of red liquorice and spear it lengthwise on the cocktail stick for the turkey's neck. Then stack a yellow sweet for the beak and a large marshmallow for the turkey's head on the cocktail stick. Use the black gel icing to dot eyes on the marshmallow.

Cut out a large feather from the card. Write 'Give thanks to God!' on the feather, and attach it to the back of the turkey with a cocktail stick.

TOE PAINTING

Kids learn that Christ sets them free from selfishness so they can serve others.

WHAT YOU'LL NEED:

You'll need a Bible, sugar paper, red, white and blue (washable) poster paint, aluminium-foil food trays, newspapers, wash basins filled with water and towels. (Suggest to girls in advance that they wear trousers and socks rather than skirts and tights to this session.)

FOR EXTRA IMPACT:

- Let each child paint their handprint and footprint on a large sheet of paper and write, 'I will use my hands and feet to serve others.'

- Ask children to write about or draw a picture of an act of service to do during the week.

WHAT TO DO

Pour different coloured paint into foil food trays. Cover the children's work area with newspapers. Older children may enjoy creating murals together, while younger children may prefer to make individual paintings.

Ask the children to take off their shoes and socks (and roll up trousers) and sit by a sheet of paper. Say: let's celebrate freedom by painting a picture with our toes. Place your toes in the trays of paint and paint a picture on your paper.

Once the children have finished their pictures, make sure they wash their feet and set the pictures aside to dry.

Ask the children to talk about their pictures. Then say: you were all free to create whatever you wanted to—with some guidelines, such as what colours to use. Let's look at another kind of freedom Christians enjoy.

Read aloud **Galatians 5:1, 13–14**. Ask: what does the Bible say Christians are free from?

Ask: what does the Bible mean when it talks about using our freedom to serve others? How can we use our freedom in Christ to serve others this week?

WISE MEN

Kids create their own 'wise men' to celebrate Christ's birth.

WHAT YOU'LL NEED:

You'll need 3 round papier-mâché craft boxes with lids (ranging in diameter from 5 cm to 20 cm) for each child. These are available at craft stores. You'll also need felt, scissors, wool, glue, poster paints, paintbrushes and various decorations.

ALLERGY ALERT
See page 10.

FOR EXTRA IMPACT:

- Bring in pictures or books showing the wise men. Let the children discuss how the wise men were all different from each other.

- Read aloud **Matthew 2:7–12**. Ask: why do you think the wise men brought gifts to Jesus? What gifts would you bring baby Jesus today?

- Fill the boxes with chocolate coins to represent the gold the wise men brought to baby Jesus.

WHAT TO DO

Give each child three round papier-mâché craft boxes of different sizes. They will stack the boxes from the largest to the smallest. Ask them to glue the bottoms of the smallest and midsize boxes to the centre of the lids of the boxes that are just a bit larger. Allow the glue to dry.

The children can decorate their boxes with paint, felt and wool to represent the wise men. Encourage them to be creative as they imagine what these men might have looked like on their visit to see Jesus. Once decorated, allow the creations to dry completely. The children can use their wise men as boxes to keep sweets in or they can give them as gifts.

CRAFTS FOR

YOUNGER CHILDREN (3-7s)

AMAZING ANIMALS

Kids love making these edible treats.

WHAT YOU'LL NEED:

You'll need chocolate mousse, small paper cups, chocolate biscuits, resealable plastic food bags, plastic spoons and animal sweets or animal biscuits. You will also need a Bible.

ALLERGY ALERT

See page 10.

FOR EXTRA IMPACT:

- Let the children take turns making the sounds of their favourite animals while the others try to guess the animal.

- Paraphrase the story of Noah's ark from **Genesis 7**. Ask the children to put pairs of matching animals in their 'dirt' cups.

WHAT TO DO

Ask the children to wash their hands. Let each child fill a small paper cup three quarters full with chocolate mousse. Give each child one chocolate biscuit. Help them to crush the chocolate biscuit inside a resealable plastic food bag. Use the chocolate biscuit crumbs to create a 'dirt' layer on top of the mousse layer. Insert animal sweets or animal biscuits in the 'dirt'.

Read aloud **Genesis 1:24–25**. Ask the children to name as many animals as they can think of. Ask them which animals are their favourite and why.

ANGEL ORNAMENTS

Kids will love making these angel ornaments for Christmas.

WHAT YOU'LL NEED:

You'll need for each ornament a white or beige shoulder pad, a wooden ball 25 mm in diameter, an 8 cm strip of pearl beading and a wool loop for the hanger. You'll also need a hot-glue gun (adult use only), tacky glue, black and red felt-tip pens, lace and trim such as sequins, buttons or rickrack.

FOR EXTRA IMPACT:

- Read aloud **Psalm 148:2**, and ask the children to repeat the verse with you.

- Ask: how do you think the angels praise God?

- Discuss ways we can praise God.

WHAT TO DO

Before the children arrive, use a hot-glue gun to attach a wooden ball to the top centre of each shoulder pad to create the head. Glue the pearl beading strip to the top of the head for the halo. Glue the wool loop on the angel's back for the hanger.

Ask the children to decorate the face with felt-tip pens. They can then use tacky glue to decorate the outside of the shoulder pad with the trim. Get them to bunch a strip of lace in the centre and glue it to the back for wings. Allow to dry.

Overlap the two tips of each shoulder pad in the front centre, and tack with a hot-glue gun. Give the children their ornaments to take home.

ANGELIC MEMORIES

Kids love making these angel keepsakes.

WHAT YOU'LL NEED:

You'll need a foam paintbrush, white poster paint in a bow, crayons or felt-tip pens, baby wipes, glue and a black or white pen. You'll also need a piece of dark-blue sugar paper and a white paper circle 5 cm in diameter for each child.

FOR EXTRA IMPACT:

- Take a picture of each child's face. Glue it on to the circle of their angel's head.

- Read aloud **Luke 2:12–14** and ask: why do the angels praise God? Why do we praise God?

WHAT TO DO

Ask each of the children to place a sheet of blue paper on a table. Help them paint their right palm white and place palm down on the paper to print the right wing of an angel. Repeat the process with the left hand. Use the baby wipes for a quick clean-up of the children's hands. Allow this part of the project to dry.

Help the children paint the bottom of one foot white. Rotate the picture 180 degrees, and place the painted foot on the blue paper between the wings, with the heel placed just above the handprints. Toes should point down to form a scalloped hem on the angel's robe.

When the paint is dry, help the children to glue a white paper circle at the top of the printed heel to form the angel's head. Let them decorate the face with crayons or felt-tip pens. Use the black or white pen to add the caption 'Our Little Angel' and the date.

CANDLE PUPPETS

Kids make candle puppets as a reminder that Jesus is the light of the world.

WHAT YOU'LL NEED:

You'll need a Bible, a kitchen-towel tube covered with yellow sugar paper, small pieces of wool, orange, yellow and red tissue-paper squares, a 4 cm precut white card flame and two googly eyes for each child. You'll also need felt-tip pens, glue, sticky tape and scissors.

FOR EXTRA IMPACT:

• Teach the children this scripture rhyme:

'I'm the light of the world.' That's what Jesus said.

With him there's no darkness, only light instead.

• Let the children march around the room waving their candle puppets as they say the rhyme.

• Ask the children to share ways we can follow Jesus' light.

WHAT TO DO

Leaving the door open for a small amount of light, turn off the lights. Ask: how would it feel to be always in the dark? Turn the lights back on and ask: does it feel better to have light? Why?

Read aloud **John 8:12**. Say: Jesus says that he is the light of the world. When we know Jesus and follow him, he brings light to our lives. Let's make candle puppets to remind us of Jesus' light in our lives.

Ask the children to glue two googly eyes on to their kitchen-towel tube. Help them draw the remainder of the face with felt-tip pens and glue on wool for the hair. The children should then scrunch the tissue-paper squares and glue them on to their card flame. After they have finished, attach each flame inside the top front of the tube using clear sticky tape. Then write each child's name on the back of his or her puppet.

CARING FOR THE SPARROW

This bird-feeder craft teaches kids how great God's love is for them and his world.

WHAT YOU'LL NEED:

You'll need a Bible, oranges, a knife (adult use only), a spoon, vegetable shortening, plastic knives, plastic straws, wool, a ruler, scissors and birdseed or popped popcorn.

ALLERGY ALERT
See page 10.

FOR EXTRA IMPACT:

- Show pictures of different birds and let children describe the different characteristics. Remind them that God made each of us special, just like the birds.

- Write the words from **Matthew 10:31b**, 'You are worth more than many sparrows,' on sheets of paper, and let the children draw pictures of their favourite birds.

- Make orange smoothies by adding the deseeded orange segments to frozen vanilla yogurt and mixing in a blender.

WHAT TO DO

Before the children arrive, cut oranges in half and carefully scoop out the orange segments with a spoon, keeping the orange peel intact. Pierce a hole on each side of each orange half about midway between the top and bottom. Place the orange segments back in the halves.

Read aloud **Matthew 10:29–31**. Give each child an orange half, and let them eat the orange segments (reminding them to watch out for pips). Help them put a straw through both holes in their orange half. Spread vegetable shortening inside the orange half and fill with birdseed or popped popcorn. Help the children thread a 25 cm piece of wool through their straw and tie the wool in a knot.

Let the children take their bird feeders home to hang in a tree. They will see their handiwork being put to use every day as they help God care for the sparrows—and other birds.

CARING HEARTS

Kids learn how Jesus loves and cares for us.

WHAT YOU'LL NEED:

You'll need red sugar paper, medium-size heart patterns, felt-tip pens, scissors, a ruler, sticky tape and a beach towel.

FOR EXTRA IMPACT:

- Children can decorate heart-shaped biscuits with red icing and talk about ways we can be like Jesus and care for each other's hearts.

ALLERGY ALERT
See page 10.

- Ask the children to talk about ways Jesus takes care of them.

WHAT TO DO

Help the children to draw and cut out three to five hearts each from red sugar paper. Help them write their name on each heart.

Spread a beach towel on the floor and ask the children to place their hearts on the towel. Get the children to hold the edges of the towel, then ask them to move the towel up and down to make the hearts bounce. Encourage the children not to let any of the hearts fall to the ground.

Ask: was it easy to keep the hearts on the towel? Why, or why not? Say: we are careful with these hearts; we don't want any of them to fall. In the same way, Jesus is careful with our hearts. He loves us, and he takes care of us.

Help the children find their hearts on the towel. Then write on their hearts sayings such as 'Jesus loves me' or 'Jesus cares for me'. Tape a 5 cm-wide strip of red sugar paper to make a crown for each child. Help the children tape their hearts to their crowns, and let them wear the crowns home.

COAT FACTORY

Kids learn about Jesus' triumphant entry into Jerusalem.

WHAT YOU'LL NEED:

You'll need a Bible, a roll of paper, a tape measure, felt-tip pens, crayons, green sugar paper and stickers.

FOR EXTRA IMPACT:

- Get the children to sit in a circle and roll a ball back and forth. The child who catches the ball should say something special about another child and then roll the ball to that child while children wave their palm branches and yell '[Child's name] is special!'

WHAT TO DO

Give each child a 75 cm length of paper with the top and bottom folded to the middle. Let the children decorate their 'coats' with felt-tip pens, crayons and stickers. As they're working, cut rounded necklines and armholes in each coat. When finished, let the children tear simple palm branches from the green sugar paper.

Get the children to wear their coats, hold their palm branches and sit in a circle.

Paraphrase **Mark 11:1–10**. Encourage the children to try out the praise words used in your text by shouting them several times. Designate one area of the room as 'Jerusalem'. Retell the story with the children acting it out.

CONCERTINA BOOKS

Kids love illustrating these fun books.

WHAT YOU'LL NEED:

You'll need A4 sheets of light-coloured, fairly thick paper (4 sheets for each child), glue sticks, scissors, cardboard and felt-tip pens.

FOR EXTRA IMPACT:

- Ask the children to form pairs and share their books with each other.

- Make a book for the group by adding more pages. Have a section for each child with a photograph and a drawing.

- Let older children make the book themselves by following along with you as you direct them step by step. Then help them to fill the book with their favourite scriptures.

WHAT TO DO

For each child, create a concertina book following these instructions. On the short side of one sheet of paper, fold back a flap about 1.5 cm wide. Then fold the rest of the sheet in half, keeping the flap folded towards the outside. Lay the folded sheet down with the flap on top.

Repeat this process with another sheet of paper. Then set the second folded sheet on top of the first sheet, slipping the bottom unfolded edge of the second sheet under the first flap. Glue the flap down over the bottom edge. Repeat these steps two more times for a concertina book that's eight pages long.

Create a cardboard heart template that's as big as, but no bigger than, the book's folded pages. Draw around this heart over the folded book's top page, keeping the folded area within the heart outline. Cut out the heart shape through all thicknesses, being careful not to cut too much of the fold.

Help children create a book with pictures of the way their family shows love to one another. Write each child's narrated words to accompany their pictures.

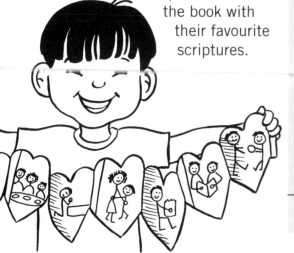

CREATION STICKY PICTURE

Kids learn about the creation story with this fun, interactive project.

WHAT YOU'LL NEED:

You'll need clear self-adhesive covering film, masking tape, sand, leaves, star confetti or small shiny star shapes, colourful feathers, pictures of animals and a picture of each child (or ask each child to draw a picture of themselves). You'll also need small squares of soft material, fabric fur, shiny yellow paper and light-blue paper.

FOR EXTRA IMPACT:

- Ask the children to talk about which part of their creation collage they like the best.

WHAT TO DO

Before the children arrive, cut out two large matching squares of self-adhesive covering film for each child. Peel the backing of the sheet, then, using masking tape, fix all four corners of this sheet, sticky side up, to the table. Reserve the matching square for the end of the project.

Tell the following creation story, and give the children the related objects. Ask them to stick the objects anywhere on the covering film in front of them.

Say: once, there was nothing, then God made light (shiny yellow square). On the second day, God made the sky (light-blue paper).

On the third day, God made land and dirt (sand). He also made water into seas or lakes. Then God made plants and fruit (leaves).

On the fourth day, God made the stars, the moon and the sun (shiny stars). On the fifth day, God made birds and fish and all their friends (feathers).

On the sixth day, God made animals. Some were furry (fabric fur) and all were very special (animal pictures). On this day, God also made people like you and me. (Give each child the picture of themselves.)

On the seventh day, God didn't make anything! He wanted to rest and give us a day to rest (soft material).

Cover the top of each picture with the matching sheet of covering film, sticky side down.

DID YOU EVER SEE...?

Kids learn about Jesus healing a blind man.

WHAT YOU'LL NEED:

You'll need a Bible, paper plates and colour-change pens.

FOR EXTRA IMPACT:

- Get half the children to walk around the room pretending to be swaying trees, while the others look through pieces of baking paper. Remove the baking paper and yell, 'I can see clearly!' Switch roles.

- Make an obstacle course using only soft items. Ask the children to form pairs, with one child wearing a blindfold while the other child carefully leads them around the course.

WHAT TO DO

Tell the children the story of the blind man at Bethsaida from **Mark 8:22–26**. Talk about how thankful the man must have been to be able to see after Jesus healed him.

Distribute paper plates and colour-change pens. Get the children to scribble a large blotch of a single colour in the middle of the paper plate. Then let them take turns using the 'colour changer' pen to draw a picture of something they're thankful for that God has made.

Ask the children to hold up their paper plates as you lead them in singing this song:

Have you ever seen a [name of picture on plate]? (Children cover their eyes.)
A [name of picture]? A [name of picture]?
Have you ever seen a [name of picture]?
And the blind man said, 'Yes!' (Children uncover their eyes and shout, 'Yes!')

Repeat the song with each child's picture. Then make a bulletin board display with the paper plates.

EDIBLE HEART ART

YOUNGER CHILDREN

Kids will love creating and eating these tasty masterpieces.

WHAT YOU'LL NEED:

Ready-rolled shortcrust pastry sheets, a large heart-shaped cookie cutter, an oven, small paper cups, a tablespoon, baking paper and thick custard. If you like, you can add red food colouring to the custard.

ALLERGY ALERT

See page 10.

FOR EXTRA IMPACT:

- Let the children fingerpaint on baking paper with any leftover custard.

- Have an art show, and let the children show off their creations before eating them.

- Read aloud **Proverbs 15:30**, and ask the children to talk about things that bring joy to their hearts.

WHAT TO DO

Before the children arrive, use a cookie cutter to cut out a heart-shaped 'canvas' from the ready-rolled pastry for each child. Bake the hearts according to the packet instructions. Prepare a thick custard according to the packet instructions and let it cool, or use ready-made custard. Add red food colouring to the custard if you'd like to. Place two tablespoons of the custard in each cup. Keep it chilled until ready to use.

Get the children to wash their hands. Give each child a cup of custard and a heart-shaped pastry 'canvas' on a sheet of baking paper. Let them fingerpaint on the 'canvases' using the custard and then eat the tasty treats.

FAITH IN BLOOM

Kids make these photo keepsakes for Valentine's Day gifts.

WHAT YOU'LL NEED:

For each child, you'll need 5 small heart cut-outs, an 8 cm card circle, a green pipe cleaner, sticky tape, a terracotta flowerpot 8 cm in diameter and a plastic-foam ball that fits in the pot. You'll also need shredded green paper, a permanent marker, glue and a wallet-size photo of each child (or ask each child to draw a picture of themselves).

FOR EXTRA IMPACT:

- Ask the children to name people who have helped their faith grow. Let them decide who they want to give their blooming photo flower to for Valentine's Day.

- Read aloud **2 Thessalonians 1:3**, and discuss ways our faith grows.

- Ask the children why they think it's important for our faith to grow.

WHAT TO DO

Ask each child to place the hearts in a circle and glue the bottom tips to the edge of the card circle. Place one end of the pipe cleaner on the circle and fix it in place with sticky tape, then glue the child's photo (or drawing) on top. Place the foam ball in the bottom of the terracotta pot. Then stick the other end of the pipe cleaner into the foam. Fill the remainder of the pot with shredded green paper. With the permanent marker, write on each child's pot: 'Happy Valentine's Day! Thanks for helping my faith bloom!'

FEELING BAG-BOOKS

Teach kids about feelings with this fun book.

WHAT YOU'LL NEED:

You'll need 7 large paper bags, felt-tip pens, a hole punch, ribbon, a ruler, scissors, 6 large resealable plastic food bags and items such as confetti, coloured paper, crayons, wrapped sweets, balloons and tissues.

ALLERGY ALERT

See page 10.

FOR EXTRA IMPACT:

- Let the children make individual Feeling Bag-Books using smaller bags.

- Ask the children to colour faces depicting four feelings on paper plates. Using a hole punch and ribbon, tie the plates together at the top.

WHAT TO DO

Lay a paper bag on a flat surface. Write 'God made feelings' across the bag, starting at the closed end of the bag and writing towards the open end of the bag.

Choose six feelings that the group would like to make a book about. Write each feeling on a different bag. Starting at the closed end of the bag and writing towards the open end, write in this form: 'I feel angry when...' or 'I feel happy when...'

Lay your seven bags on top of each other and punch two holes in the closed ends of the bags about 2 cm from the edge and 8 cm apart. Cut a 20 cm piece of ribbon and thread it through the holes. Tie a bow in the ribbon on the title side.

Say: look through these items and choose things that represent these feelings. For example, you may choose a balloon and confetti for when you're happy. Put the items together in a plastic food bag and put it in the paper bag labelled with that feeling.

Read aloud the paper-bag book. As you read each feeling, take out the plastic bag and let the children explain why they chose their items.

FOOTPRINTS KEEPSAKE

Kids can make this special keepsake for Mother's Day or Father's Day.

WHAT YOU'LL NEED:

You'll need A4 pieces of paper with a copy of 'My Footprints' (on this page) in the centre, washable paint, ribbon, a marker pen and a water basin and towels for the clean-up.

FOR EXTRA IMPACT:

- Provide banner paper, and ask each child to make a set of footprints on it. As the children look at the footprints, talk about how God made each one of us different. Write on the banner, 'Our footprints follow Jesus.' Then display it on the wall.

- Read aloud **Luke 18:22**, and discuss ways we can follow Jesus.

WHAT TO DO

Give each child a copy of 'My Footprints'. Help the children make washable-paint footprints on their poems. When the footprints have dried, write each child's name on his or her poem, roll the paper like a scroll, and tie with a ribbon.

My Footprints

When I was just a baby,
My footprints were really small.
I could not walk anywhere.
You carried me proud and tall.

Now that I am bigger,
My footprints are big, too.
I can run, walk, gallop, skip;
But I still need you.

I need your guidance and your love
To keep my footprints placed
On paths where I will learn what's right
And seek God's love and grace.

Some day when I grow up,
I hope you will look back
To think of times when I was small
And be proud of my feet's path.

GLITTER JARS

These glittery jars will remind kids of the goodness of God's creation.

WHAT YOU'LL NEED:

You'll need a Bible, baby-food jars with lids, small artificial flower blossoms, clay, water, glitter and nail polish.

FOR EXTRA IMPACT:

• For added sparkle, add foil confetti to the jars.

• For a fun, ocean-like effect, add a couple of drops of blue food colouring to the jars.

• Teach the children this prayer to say as they shake their jars:

Thank you, God, for the world you made. May I see your goodness every day.

WHAT TO DO

Help the children to press clay on to the inside of a baby-food jar lid and stick artificial flower blossoms into the clay. Fill the jars almost to the top with water and let the children drop in a few pinches of glitter. Screw the lids on to the jars, and paint around the edges of the lids with nail polish to seal the lids. Allow to dry. Let the children shake the jars and then set them on the lids.

As the glitter swirls around in the water, ask: how did you feel as you made your small world that glitters? How do you think God felt when he made the world?

Read aloud **Genesis 1:31**. Say: God saw all that he had made, and it was good. What do you think is good about your jar? What do you think about God's creation?

GLUE AND GLITTER BUTTERFLIES

Kids learn about becoming new creations in Christ.

WHAT YOU'LL NEED:

You'll need a Bible, glue, glue spreaders, wax paper, glitter, a box lid and nylon thread or string.

FOR EXTRA IMPACT:

- Ask the children to crouch down on the floor and pretend to be caterpillars, and then pop up and flutter around the room like butterflies, shouting, 'I'm a new creation in Christ!'

- Let the children make a small butterfly to take home. Place double-sided sticky tape around the edges of precut sugar-paper butterfly shapes. Sprinkle on glitter and add pipe cleaners for the antennae.

- Make small butterflies and tie them on a coat hanger with wool to make a mobile.

WHAT TO DO

Help the children 'paint' a simple butterfly shape on a sheet of wax paper with the glue. Make sure that each butterfly body is filled in with glue. Make the outline of the wing sections at least 1.5 cm thick.

Shake assorted colours of glitter over the glue, making sure the glue is completely covered. Gently lift the wax paper, and shake the excess glitter back into the glitter container or a box lid for future use.

Set the wax paper aside for several days to let the glue and glitter dry. When it's completely dry, carefully peel the butterfly shape from the paper.

At the next session, help the children thread a length of nylon thread or string through each butterfly. Hang the butterflies from the ceiling where they can blow in the breeze!

Read aloud **2 Corinthians 5:17**. Say: when a caterpillar becomes a butterfly, it is a new creation. The Bible says when we are in Christ, we become new creations. Ask: what is one thing about you that shows that you are a new creation in Christ?

Close in prayer, thanking God for the new life that's available through Jesus' death and resurrection.

I CAN PRAY

Kids learn about prayer.

WHAT YOU'LL NEED:

You'll need sugar paper, stickers, glitter, crayons and empty plastic containers with lids.

FOR EXTRA IMPACT:

- Ask the children to form pairs, share their drawings with each other, and pray together by saying a simple prayer, such as 'Help us, God.'

- Challenge them to take their containers home and pray for their requests every day.

- Let the children make another container to fill with paper strips on which they've drawn things they're thankful for. Encourage them to use these to give thanks to God every day.

WHAT TO DO

Give each child a plastic container that you've covered with sugar paper. On each container, write 'I CAN PRAY'. Let the children decorate their containers with stickers, glitter and crayons.

Give each child four small pieces of paper. Ask them to draw a picture of something they want to pray for on each piece of paper. Suggest praying for their parents, your church or people who are sick. Get the children to fold their drawings and put them into their containers. During prayer time, encourage them to pull out pictures and pray for what they've drawn.

INCREDIBLE EDIBLE SCULPTURE

Kids will have fun making edible sculptures and learning how God made each of us different.

WHAT YOU'LL NEED:

You'll need resealable plastic bags, 225 g cream cheese, 1 tablespoon of honey, 60 g dried skimmed milk powder, a fridge, paper plates, Smarties®, mini-marshmallows, red liquorice laces and desiccated coconut.

ALLERGY ALERT

See page 10.

FOR EXTRA IMPACT:

- Ask the children to sit in a circle and share something special about the child to their right.

- Take photos of the children with their sculptures to put on a bulletin board in the room.

- Give the children a copy of the rhyme to take home.

WHAT TO DO

Fill a resealable plastic bag with the cream cheese, the dried skimmed milk powder and the honey. Seal the bag, and squeeze it to mix the ingredients until smooth. One bag will supply enough dough for five children. Keep the dough refrigerated until you need it; because cream cheese is perishable, it is advisable to make the dough on the day you intend to use it, and discard unused dough after the activity.

Ask the children to wash their hands, then give each child a small ball of the edible dough on a paper plate. Help each child knead the dough, press it into a circle and then make a face using Smarties® and mini marshmallows for the eyes and nose, red liquorice laces for the mouth and desiccated coconut for the hair.

Before the children eat their sculptures, ask them to look at each other's creations. Ask: do you see any that look exactly alike? Does God make any two people exactly alike?

Lead the children in the words and actions to this rhyme:

God made you. (Point to someone.)
God made me. (Point to yourself.)
We're all different (Point to everyone.)
In God's family. (Point up and then cross your arms over your chest.)

LIFEBELTS

Kids learn that Jesus is their lifesaver.

YOUNGER CHILDREN

WHAT YOU'LL NEED:

You'll need a Bible, yellow card, scissors, a ruler, sand, washable non-toxic powder paint, glue, glue spreaders, shells and chairs.

FOR EXTRA IMPACT:

- Let the children talk about things that make them afraid. Get the other children to respond by saying, 'Don't be afraid! Jesus is with you!'

- Encourage the children to pray to thank Jesus for always being with us so we never have to be afraid.

WHAT TO DO

Before the children arrive, cut yellow card circles approximately 60 cm in diameter. You'll need one for each child. Cut out the centre of the circle so it's large enough to fit around a child's waist. Slice the circle to make an opening. Make coloured sand by adding dry powder paint to sand.

Help each of the children to decorate a 'lifebelt' by painting glue on a card circle and sprinkling it with coloured sand. They can glue on small shells.

Then say: we're going to take a boat ride. To help keep us safe, we need to put on our lifebelts. Lifebelts help us float if we fall into the water.

Use chairs to form a 'boat'. Get the children to sit in the boat. Read aloud **Matthew 8:23–27.** Encourage the children to act out sea motions by waving their arms and to make wind sounds by rubbing their hands together and blowing through their mouths.

Ask: why were Jesus' friends afraid? Have you ever been afraid? Why, or why not? How would you have felt if you were in the boat with Jesus? How do you think Jesus' friends felt when the boat stopped rocking?

Say: with Jesus, we don't have to be afraid because he's always with us.

MARSHMALLOW SHEEP

Kids have fun making edible sheep.

WHAT YOU'LL NEED:

You'll need large and miniature marshmallows, white icing, red liquorice or strawberry laces, a tube of blue icing, plastic knives and paper plates.

ALLERGY ALERT
See page 10.

FOR EXTRA IMPACT:

- Read aloud **Luke 15:3–7**, and let the children act out the story. Ask them to take turns being the lost sheep and the shepherd.

- Ask children who have lost a pet and then found it to talk about how the experience felt and why.

- Read aloud **Psalm 23**, and ask: in what ways is God our shepherd? How can we follow him?

WHAT TO DO

Ask the children to wash their hands. Give each child a paper plate and two large marshmallows for the sheep's body and one large marshmallow for the head. Use miniature marshmallows for legs and a tail. Cut one miniature marshmallow in half vertically, and place one half on each side of the sheep's head for ears.

Use white icing to connect all the marshmallows. Dot on the sheep's eyes using the blue icing, and create its mouth using liquorice or strawberry laces, attached with white icing.

MARVELLOUS HELPERS

Kids learn about helping their parents just as Miriam did.

WHAT YOU'LL NEED:

You'll need a Bible, painting aprons, white sugar paper, poster paint, paintbrushes, self-adhesive covering film, a hairdryer, a slotted turner, a fabric-softener lid, cookie cutters, a small whisk, a sponge and an old toothbrush.

FOR EXTRA IMPACT:

- Challenge the children to find one thing they can do every day to help their parents.

- Make a play area where the children can act out the story of Miriam watching Moses from the bulrushes. Use a blue blanket for the water, leafy potted plants for reeds and a doll in a basket for the baby.

- Play 'Mummy Says' or 'Daddy Says' instead of Simon Says. Use commands such as 'Mummy says make your bed,' or 'Wash the dishes,' and let the children pretend to make their beds and wash dishes.

WHAT TO DO

Give each child a sheet of sugar paper. Help them to use poster paint to make prints on their paper with a slotted turner, a fabric-softener lid, cookie cutters, a small whisk, a sponge and an old toothbrush. Allow the papers to dry.

Ask: how can you use some of these items to help your parents at home? What other ways do you help your parents? Say: let's hear a story about how Miriam helped her mother.

Paraphrase **Exodus 2:1–10** to tell the story of Moses' sister Miriam watching baby Moses from the reeds. Ask: what did Miriam do to help her mother? How do you think Miriam felt as she helped her mother? How do you feel when you help your parents?

At the end of the session, get an adult to use a hairdryer to finish drying any wet paint. Then cover the papers with self-adhesive covering film so the children can give them to their parents as place mats.

PHOTO BOUQUETS

Kids make treasured photo keepsakes.

WHAT YOU'LL NEED:

You'll need 6 photos of each child, card, sticky tape, glue, scissors, green craft sticks, small pots and floral foam.

FOR EXTRA IMPACT:

- Let the children decorate terracotta pots with paint and ribbon to hold their photo bouquets.

- Read aloud **Proverbs 18:16**, and ask the children why we give gifts.

- Discuss how it feels to receive gifts and how it feels to give gifts to others.

WHAT TO DO

Help the children create gifts for their parents and grandparents that will be treasured for years. In advance, take six photos of each child so you can have them printed for this craft. Alternatively, ask the children to bring in six photos of themselves that you can cut up.

From card, cut out flower and leaf shapes. Help the children to cut out their pictures and glue them to the centre of their flowers. Then use tape on the back of the flowers and leaves to attach them to green craft sticks. Children can then arrange their flowers in small pots with floral foam in the bottom.

PRAISE KAZOOS

Kids make instruments to praise Jesus.

WHAT YOU'LL NEED:

You'll need kitchen-towel tubes, rubber bands, 10 cm squares of baking paper and a straightened paper clip (for adult use only).

FOR EXTRA IMPACT:

- Read aloud **Psalm 150:3**, and ask: How do you think Jesus feels when we praise him?

- Let the children decorate their kazoos with felt-tip pens and stickers.

- Have a praise parade, and let the children march around and play their kazoos.

WHAT TO DO

Give each child a kitchen-towel tube, a rubber band and a 10 cm square of baking paper. Use the rubber band to hold the baking paper on one end of the tube. Get an adult to use the paper clip to poke holes in the baking paper. Let the children put the open end of the tube to their lips and rehearse by singing these words to the tune of 'Yankee Doodle'.

Verse: *Jesus Christ, he came to town, a-riding on a donkey. Jesus came to be my King, and that's why I am singing.*

Chorus: *Jesus Christ came to town, came to be my Saviour. Jesus Christ came to town. I'm so glad that he loves me!*

RAINDROPS AND MUD PLOPS

Kids learn about how rain helps plants grow.

WHAT YOU'LL NEED:

You'll need brown non-toxic finger paint, blue sugar paper, felt-tip pens, scissors, glue and baby wipes for the clean-up. You'll also need to copy the poem (on this page) on to A4 white paper for each child.

FOR EXTRA IMPACT:

- Read the poem aloud, and ask the children how they feel when it's stormy.

- Ask: what can you do when you're afraid?

- Close in prayer, thanking God for the rain and asking him to help children remember not to be afraid during storms.

WHAT TO DO

Before the children arrive, copy this poem on to a piece of A4 paper for each child:

*When the lightning strikes
and the thunder roars,
Don't be afraid,
but go quickly indoors.
For it is God's plan, you see,
Not to scare or frighten me.
The plants need water—just like me!*

Let the children use brown finger paint to make muddy fingerprints on the bottom of their paper. While the fingerprints dry, help the children cut out large blue raindrops from the sugar paper and glue them around the poem. Then they can use felt-tip pens to colour flowers on top of the dry fingerprints.

Discuss how rain helps plants to grow. Then brainstorm other ways that rain is helpful.

When the lightning strikes
and the thunder roars,
Don't be afraid,
but go quickly indoors.
For it is God's plan, you see,
Not to scare or frighten me.
The plants need water—
just like me!

SWEET BIBLE SNACK

Kids make snacks to remind them that God's word is sweet.

YOUNGER CHILDREN

WHAT YOU'LL NEED:

You'll need napkins, paper plates, plastic knives, rectangular biscuits, white icing, black and red sprinkles, red liquorice or strawberry laces and a Bible that shows Jesus' words in red.

ALLERGY ALERT

See page 10.

FOR EXTRA IMPACT:

- Read aloud **Matthew 4:2–4,** and ask: how can our hearts be fed by God's word?

- Before the children eat, ask them to say a blessing to thank God for his word and for the Sweet Bible Snacks.

WHAT TO DO

Say: the Bible is a special book because God talks to us through the Bible.

Open your Bible to one of the Gospels, show the children a passage, and say: the Bible says that God's promises are sweet to us. Most of the words in the Bible are black, but in this copy of the Bible, Jesus' words are red.

Give each child a paper plate and napkin. Help them to spread the icing on their biscuit. Then get them to put some black and red sprinkles on top. Finally, add a red liquorice 'bookmark' to the middle of the Bible snacks.

Say: the black sprinkles remind us of words in the Bible, and the red sprinkles remind us of Jesus' words in red. Let's thank God for this sweet snack that reminds us of how good the Bible is. Then let's eat!

VALENTINE FAN

Kids will love these handmade creations for Mum, Dad or other special people.

WHAT YOU'LL NEED:

You'll need plain paper, a pen, sugar paper, white card, red and pink crayons, a stapler, pink or red poster paint, glue, washing-up liquid, sponges, jumbo craft sticks, sticky tape, a basin of water and towels.

FOR EXTRA IMPACT:

- Let the children march around the room to music while waving their valentine fans.

- Ask the children to talk about special people they love.

WHAT TO DO

At the top of a sheet of paper, draw a heart outline and write 'Jesus loves you!' in it. At the top of another sheet of paper, draw a heart outline and write 'I love you, too!' in it. You could write the name of your church and the date at the bottom of this second paper. For each child, photocopy each paper on to white card.

Let the children colour their valentines with red and pink crayons. You could add each child's name.

Mix pink or red poster paint with washing-up liquid for easier clean-up. Spread the paint on a sponge. Lay out each child's valentine face up. Get each child to press their hand into the paint on the sponge and then make a handprint on each card. Re-apply paint between handprints. Messy hands can go straight into a basin of warm water that you've set on a thick towel.

After the paint has dried, place the two sheets of card back to back, and staple them together at the top edges. Tape a jumbo craft-stick 'handle' between the two sheets of card at the bottom, and glue the edges together.

CRAFTS FOR

OLDER CHILDREN (7-11s)

BEARING FRUIT

Kids make encouraging cards for their parents.

WHAT YOU'LL NEED:

You'll need a Bible, packets of fruit or vegetable seeds, card, felt-tip pens and glue.

FOR EXTRA IMPACT:

- Encourage the children to plant the seeds at home with their parents.

- Let the children make a colourful bulletin board. Write 'We plant seeds for Jesus,' and decorate with seed packets and sugar-paper flowers. For added effect, glue a picture of each child in the centre of each flower.

- Read aloud **Galatians 5:22–23,** and let the children choose one fruit of the Spirit and share one way they can show that quality to others.

WHAT TO DO

Give each child a packet of fruit or vegetable seeds and a sheet of card. Ask a child to read aloud **Galatians 5:22–23** about the fruit of the Spirit. Talk about these scriptures as the children fold their card in half to make cards.

On the front page of the cards, the children can write a message for their parents. Inside the cards on the right-hand side, get the children to glue their seed packets. On the inside left-hand page of each card, ask the children to write the words from **Galatians 5:22–23**. Then get the children to sign their cards and give them to their parents.

OLDER CHILDREN

BIBLE FISH

Kids make a colourful display of the Easter story.

WHAT YOU'LL NEED:

You'll need an even number of large, precut paper fish shapes (at least 1 per child), a stapler, tissue paper, felt-tip pens, sugar paper, glue, sticker name tags, wool and various craft supplies.

FOR EXTRA IMPACT:

- Let the pairs read their Bible passage aloud and show their fish to the group.

- Hang the fish in order of the passages, and attach the scripture verses for a chronological display of the Easter story.

WHAT TO DO

Before the children arrive, print these portions of the Easter story on paper: Jesus' arrest (**Luke 22:47–54**); Jesus before Pilate (**Luke 23:1–7**); Jesus before Herod (**Luke 23:8–25**); Simon bears the cross (**Luke 23:26–31**); the crucifixion (**Luke 23:33–49**); Jesus' burial (**Luke 23:50–56**); the resurrection (**Luke 24:1–12**); the road to Emmaus (**Luke 24:13–35**); and the ascension (**Luke 24:50–53**).

Get the children to work with a partner. Give each pair one Bible passage. They should read the verses and decide how they can decorate their fish to illustrate this part of Easter.

Let the children use the craft materials to decorate their fish. Then they can sign a name tag and stick it on their fish to show who did the great artwork. Ask them to staple both sides of their fish together, leaving an opening, stuff tissue paper through the opening and then staple the fish shut.

Afterwards, use wool to hang the fish from the ceiling for everyone to enjoy.

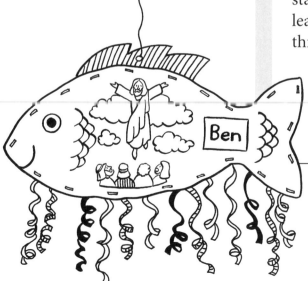

CHURCH MOUSE MATS

Kids can design their own mouse mats with this quick and easy activity.

WHAT YOU'LL NEED:

You'll need sheets of craft foam in assorted colours (ideally 23 cm x 19 cm), sheets of sticky-back craft foam that are the same size as the other foam sheets, pencils and scissors.

FOR EXTRA IMPACT:

- Bring in pictures of Christian symbols for the children to see. Explain what the different symbols mean.

- Ask each child to show the class their mouse mat, and explain why they picked that symbol.

- Let the children use felt-tip pens or paint pens to write their favourite scripture verses on their mouse mats.

WHAT TO DO

Give each child a sheet of sticky-back craft foam. Ask them to choose two differently coloured sheets of non-sticky craft foam.

Get them to cut out a Christian symbol, such as a cross, fish, crown or heart, from one of the non-sticky craft-foam sheets. The symbol must fit inside the other non-sticky sheet of craft foam.

The children should then draw around the symbol on to the other sheet of non-sticky craft foam and carefully cut it out. They can press the cut-out into the stencil, creating a contrasting design. Peel the backing off the sticky-back craft foam and then carefully place the sticky side on the bottom of the craft foam design, matching the edges.

FATHER'S DAY HOUSE

Kids make paper houses with special treats for their fathers or special adult males in their lives.

WHAT YOU'LL NEED:

You'll need a Bible, A4 sheets of white card, small resealable food bags, scissors, double-sided sticky tape, crayons, felt-tip pens, large stickers and small wrapped sweets.

ALLERGY ALERT

See page 10.

FOR EXTRA IMPACT:

- Read aloud **Exodus 20:12**, and ask what it means to 'honour your father'.

- Challenge the children to pick one thing to do during the week to honour their dads.

WHAT TO DO

Before you begin, draw the diagram (below) on a sheet of card. Write the words and reference from **Joshua 24:15** on each door to the right of the doorknob. Photocopy the diagram on to card. Each sheet of card makes two houses. Cut the card in half along the solid centre line. Make a model house for the children to see.

Ask the children to turn the card face down and fold back along the dotted lines. Set the house on its base, and fold the top flap over the back flap. Then unfold. The children can use felt-tip pens and crayons to decorate the front of the house.

Fill a resealable food bag with small sweets and close it. Using double-sided sticky tape, attach the bag to the inside of the house just below the top fold. Refold the top flap, and secure it to the back flap with a large sticker.

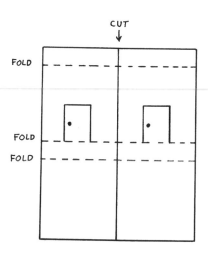

FISHER OF PEOPLE PIN

Kids can share their faith with their friends with this creative craft.

WHAT YOU'LL NEED:

You'll need a Bible, scissors, fine-tipped black permanent markers and thick tacky or craft-foam glue. For each pin, you'll need a 2.5 cm x 9 cm strip of craft foam, any colour, a 5 cm square of white craft foam and a 4 cm jewellery pin attachment.

FOR EXTRA IMPACT:

- Cut cardboard patterns of banners and hooks for the children to draw around on the craft foam.

- Give each child a piece of netting. Ask them to cut people shapes out of the craft foam to glue on to the netting and then to attach a paper tag to the net with the words 'I'm a fisher of people for Jesus.'

- Ask the children to list ways they can share their faith with their friends during the following week, using the pins as conversation-starters. Get them to report back next week with their faith-sharing stories.

WHAT TO DO

Ask the children to cut mini banners out of the coloured craft foam and hook shapes from the white craft foam. Glue the hook on the pointed end of the banner shape. Write 'Fisher of People' down the length of the banner. Glue the pin to the back of the banner. Allow the glue to dry before wearing.

Read aloud **Matthew 4:18–20**. Ask: what does it mean to be fishers of people? What are ways we can follow Jesus?

Close in prayer, asking Jesus to help the children share their faith with others so they can be fishers of people like Peter and Andrew.

GOOD NEWS TULIPS

Kids make tulips as a reminder that Jesus is always with us.

WHAT YOU'LL NEED:

You'll need a Bible, precut 10 cm x 13 cm pieces of red, pink, blue and white felt, glue, ribbon, glitter, scissors, a ruler, staplers, green pipe cleaners, small plastic sandwich bags, mixed dried fruit, yellow paper strips and fine-tipped permanent markers.

ALLERGY ALERT

See page 10.

FOR EXTRA IMPACT:

- Reread aloud **Matthew 28:20**, and ask: how does it feel to know Jesus is with us always?

- Ask the children to pray by name for the person they will give their Good News Tulip to and to ask God to help them always feel Jesus' presence.

WHAT TO DO

Read aloud **Matthew 28:1–8**. Say: it may have been dark inside the tomb, but it really was a place of great joy! Ask the children to layer three 10 cm x 13 cm pieces of the same colour felt and cut the layers into a 10 cm-tall and 8 cm-wide egg shape. Take the top egg off the stack and staple the two stacked pieces along the right edge, leaving the top quarter open, as shown in the illustration.

Fold both these pieces in half towards the stapled outer edge. Lay the third piece on top of the sections of the other two that have been folded back, matching the open edges, and staple the third piece to the other two. Again leave the top quarter open. The trio of egg shapes forms a tulip bud. Trim the bottom of the tulip to get it to stand up.

Decorate the outside of the tulip with glitter and ribbon. Form leaves at the base with green pipe cleaners.

As the glue dries, fill sandwich bags with dried fruit and tie them with ribbons. Place them inside the tulips. Write "'I am with you always"—Matthew 28:20' on the yellow paper strips, and place them inside the tulips. Ask children to give their Good News Tulips to friends and neighbours.

HARVEST CROSS

Kids make a harvest cross to mark the changing seasons.

OLDER CHILDREN

WHAT YOU'LL NEED:

You'll need a Bible, 10 small or medium pine cones per child, dried or artificial autumn leaves, ribbon, craft wire, cardboard, scissors, a hot-glue gun (adult use only) and craft glue.

FOR EXTRA IMPACT:

- Ask the children to write '"There is a time for everything, and a season for every activity under the heavens"—Ecclesiastes 3:1' on a tag and attach it to the cross hanger.

- Ask: what's most special to you about this season? What can we enjoy and thank God for at this time of year?

- Ask the children to bring in old school photos from different years to display on a bulletin board. As they look at the photos, talk about how people change just as seasons do.

WHAT TO DO

Before the children arrive, cut out a cardboard cross for each child to use as backing. Make a small hole at the top of the cross for the wire hanger. Using a hot-glue gun, glue the pine cones to the cardboard backing with the pointed ends up. Leave space in the middle of the cross. Allow the glue to cool.

Read aloud **Ecclesiastes 3:1–8**. Ask the children: why do you think God made seasons? How do our lives change like the seasons? To celebrate this season, we're going to make a harvest cross.

Let the children use craft glue to fix the leaves to the central part of the cross, then tie a ribbon bow and glue it on top of the leaf arrangement. Finally, make a wire loop for a hanger and thread it through the hole at the top of the cross.

HEART FULL OF THANKS

Kids make gifts to say thanks to those who teach them about God.

WHAT YOU'LL NEED:

You'll need a Bible, 22 cm x 28 cm pieces of red felt (2 for each child), another colour of felt, glue, scissors, a ruler, fabric pens, pencils, wrapped chocolates (heart-shaped if possible), notecards and a fine-tipped permanent marker.

ALLERGY ALERT

See page 10.

FOR EXTRA IMPACT:

- Ask the children to sit in a circle and place the leftover chocolates in the middle. As they say ways they can touch someone's heart, let them receive a chocolate for each way they name.

- Read aloud **Philippians 1:3**. Ask the children to name people they're thankful for and say why.

- Ask the children to pray and thank God for each person named.

WHAT TO DO

Stack two pieces of 22 cm x 28 cm red felt. Fold one felt piece in half, then draw one half of a heart along the fold, making it as large as will fit on the felt. Cut out the heart. Cut the second piece of felt in the same way.

Outline the border of one heart with glue, leaving an 8 cm section at the top dry. Lay the second heart on top of the first, matching the edges. Outline one hand on a piece of different colour felt and cut it out. Attach the felt hand to the heart with glue.

Once the glue is dry, use fabric pens to write 'You touch my heart' on the side without the hand.

Fill the heart with chocolates. Write the words of **Philippians 1:3** on a notecard, and put it in the heart. Children can give the hearts to church or children's leaders.

JONAH AND THE RAGING SEA

Kids will love this interactive craft project.

WHAT YOU'LL NEED:

You'll need a Bible, empty plastic 2-litre bottles with lids, water, green and blue food colouring, vegetable oil, a measuring jug, margarine-tub lids, scissors, permanent markers, aluminium foil, small shells, glue and sticky tape.

FOR EXTRA IMPACT:

- Use clear nail polish to paint around the edges of the lid instead of using tape and glue. Allow to dry for a quick seamless seal.

- Ask the children to form pairs and take turns using their sea bottles to tell the story of Jonah to each other.

- Get the children to sit in a circle, place a sea bottle in the middle and take turns spinning the bottle. When the bottle stops, let the child it points to roll into the middle of the circle, as if being tossed by the waves, and yell 'Lord save us from the raging sea!'

WHAT TO DO

Before the session, use warm water to remove the labels from the bottles. Ask each child to fill their plastic bottle about two-thirds full of water. Add a few drops of food colouring and 60 ml of vegetable oil. Cut fish shapes and a Jonah figure from margarine-tub lids. They need to fit into the bottle opening. Use permanent markers to decorate them, then push them into the bottle.

Roll aluminium foil into balls and other shapes. Place these shapes and the shells in the water. Use glue and sticky tape to secure the bottle top. Roll or shake the bottle on its side to see a raging sea with Jonah swimming for his life.

Paraphrase the story from **Jonah 1:1–16**. Ask: how do you think Jonah felt when he was thrown into the water? What would you have prayed if you had been Jonah? Have you ever been in a hopeless situation and tried praying about it? Explain. How did God answer your prayer?

OLDER CHILDREN

LAST DAYS JOURNAL

Kids make journals to learn about some of the events in Jesus' last week.

WHAT YOU'LL NEED:

You'll need plain A4 paper, sugar paper, a stapler, felt-tip pens and crayons.

FOR EXTRA IMPACT:

- Let the children form small groups to share their favourite entry from their journal.

- They could also make a family journal. Family members can take turns writing entries in it at home.

- Include blank pages in the journal, and encourage the children to continue to write and draw in their journals after Easter.

WHAT TO DO

Print the following entries and scripture references on separate pages.

Sunday—Entering Jerusalem (Mark 11:1–10)

Monday—Judas' plot against Jesus (Matthew 26:1–16)

Tuesday—Eats Last Supper (Matthew 26:26–30)

Wednesday—Gethsemane (Matthew 26:36–46); betrayed and arrested (Luke 22:47–65)

Thursday—Tried by Jewish authorities (Matthew 27:11–31); tried by Pilate (John 19:1–16)

Friday—Crucifixion (Matthew 27:32–54); burial (Matthew 27:57–61)

Saturday—Guarding the tomb (Matthew 27:62–66)

Sunday—Empty tomb (Matthew 28:1–8); appearing to disciples (Luke 24:36–48)

Photocopy enough pages for each child to have a complete set. Make journals by stapling a set of pages between two sheets of sugar paper. Let the children decorate their journal covers. They could also draw pictures on each page.

Let the children take their journals home and read the scriptures with their families on the appropriate day during the week before Easter.

OLDER CHILDREN

MYSTERY CROSS

Kids learn about God's forgiveness.

WHAT YOU'LL NEED:

You'll need red plastic film, scissors, a red pencil, a normal writing pencil and white paper.

FOR EXTRA IMPACT:

- Read aloud **Ephesians 1:7**. Ask the children to write on the white paper above the cross 'God forgives my sins.'

- Ask the children what it means to them that God forgives their sins.

- Ask them to sit in silence and think of something they've done that they want God to forgive. Then close in prayer with everyone saying aloud, 'God forgives us for our sins.'

WHAT TO DO

Ask the children to cut their film into the shape of a cross. Use the red pencil to write 'sin' on white paper and then write 'forgiveness' in normal pencil. Make sure the words fit within the borders of the cross.

Cover 'forgiveness' with red pencil dots or scribbles so the word can't be easily read. Slide the red film over the paper and watch 'sin' disappear and 'forgiveness' shine through.

Explain to the children how Jesus died to take our sin away and replace it with God's forgiveness.

OLDER CHILDREN

NATIVITY ORNAMENT

Kids make this aromatic nativity ornament to celebrate Christmas.

WHAT YOU'LL NEED:

You'll need a 15 cm length of ribbon, 5 cinnamon sticks and a small wooden or cardboard star for each child. You'll also need yellow paint, paintbrushes, glitter, Christmas cards with nativity scenes or a nativity scene rubber stamp, coloured pencils and paper, scissors, potpourri and glue.

FOR EXTRA IMPACT:

- Bring in different nativity scenes for children to see.

- Let the children create a nativity scene in the room using boxes, dolls, soft animal toys and other props.

- Read aloud **Luke 2:4–7**, and ask the children how Joseph and Mary may have felt when there was no room in the inn.

WHAT TO DO

Let each child paint a small wooden star with yellow paint and sprinkle glitter over the wet paint. Allow the paint to dry. Glue five cinnamon sticks into the shape of a house.

As the glue on the house dries, create a nativity scene by cutting out the nativity figures on a Christmas card, drawing the figures on paper or cutting out a rubber-stamped nativity scene on a sheet of paper. Glue the nativity scene to the dried cinnamon-stick stable.

Glue potpourri on to the sides of the stable for a rustic look—and nice smell. Then glue the star to the top of the stable. Insert a 15 cm piece of ribbon through the top of the stable, and tie the ribbon to serve as a hanger.

ON MY HEART NECKLACE

Kids learn about keeping God's word close to their hearts.

WHAT YOU'LL NEED:

You'll need air-hardening clay, a pencil, wool, heart-shaped cookie cutters, rolling pins and felt-tip pens.

FOR EXTRA IMPACT:

- Read aloud **Psalm 119:11**. Ask the children what it means to hide God's word in their hearts.

- Make a list of ways we can keep God's word in our hearts. Challenge the children to pick one thing from that list to do during the week.

- Let the children make an extra necklace for a friend. Wrap it in tissue paper, tie with wool and attach a tag with the words of **Psalm 119:11**.

WHAT TO DO

Get the children to make a necklace as a reminder to keep God's teachings close to their hearts. They can do this by moulding the clay into a heart shape, or by rolling out the clay and cutting out a heart shape using a cookie cutter. Help the children to use a pencil to pierce an opening through the top of their heart shapes and to carve 'God's word' on to them. Let the clay harden according to the packet instructions.

When the clay is ready, the children can decorate their heart shapes using felt-tip pens. Thread and knot the wool for the necklace 'chain'.

PEACEFUL MAGNETISM

Kids make fridge magnets to learn about peace.

WHAT YOU'LL NEED:

You'll need a roll of flexible magnetic tape (around 1.5 cm wide), yellow 23 cm x 15 cm craft-foam sheets, a pencil, ruler, scissors and puffy fabric paint.

FOR EXTRA IMPACT:

- Ask the children to write the words to the acrostic on a sheet of sugar paper and decorate with felt-tip pens. They can put the reminder on their fridge with their letter magnets.

- Discuss ways we can be Christ's example to others.

- Read aloud **2 Corinthians 5:20**, and ask why it's important for us to be Christ's ambassadors of peace to the world.

WHAT TO DO

Using a ruler as a guide, lightly draw large block letters on the foam sheets so that the letters spell 'peace'. Cut out the letters and decorate the front of the letters with fabric paint. Once the paint is dry, peel and place the adhesive side of the magnetic strip on the back of the letters.

Teach the children this acrostic for the letters: People Everywhere Acting out Christ's Example. Let them take their letters home to hang on their fridges.

PILLOW PRESENTS

Kids can make special gifts for others.

WHAT YOU'LL NEED:

You'll need washed and ironed plain pillowcases, fabric paint, paintbrushes, fabric pens and cardboard. Alternatively, poster paint can be used to decorate large paper bags.

FOR EXTRA IMPACT:

- Let the children make their own pillowcase keepsakes, writing their favourite verse of scripture on them.
- Read aloud **Ephesians 2:8**, and discuss the gift that God has given us.

For it is by grace you have been saved, through faith— and this is not from yourselves, it is the gift of God. Ephesians 2:8

WHAT TO DO

Ask each child to place a piece of cardboard in their pillowcase, then decorate the pillowcase using fabric paints. Leave space in the centre for a message.

Let the children decide who they want to give their pillowcase to, then get them to write a suitable message in the centre using fabric pens.

Suggested gift ideas:

For new mothers: 'Welcome! From your friends at church!' Fill the pillowcase with baby gifts.

For teachers, children's leaders or the church leader: 'Thanks for teaching us!' Fill with a box of chocolates and other edible treats.

(Include with the gift a slip of paper giving washing instructions, as per the instructions on the fabric paint packet.)

ALLERGY ALERT
See page 10.

POINTED REMINDER

Kids make these cross necklaces as a reminder of Jesus' sacrifice.

WHAT YOU'LL NEED:

You'll need a Bible, long and short nails, fine-gauge wire and nylon cord.

FOR EXTRA IMPACT:

- Ask: how does it feel to know that Christ died for your sins?

- Encourage the children to each hold their cross and think about their sins that Jesus died for. Close with each child offering a prayer of thanks to Jesus.

- Let the children make extra necklaces to share Jesus' love with others.

WHAT TO DO

Say: for Christians, Good Friday is the most solemn day of the year because it's the day we remember the suffering and death of Jesus. Read aloud **Matthew 27:33–50**. Say: Jesus died for us so we can have eternal life. To help us remember Christ's death for us, let's make a cross necklace.

Give each child four nails, two of which are a little shorter than the other two. Lay the two long nails head to point next to each other. Similarly, lay the two shorter nails across the long nails to form a cross. Bind them together with fine-gauge wire, and suspend the cross on a nylon cord to make a necklace. The necklaces can remind the children of Jesus' sacrifice for us.

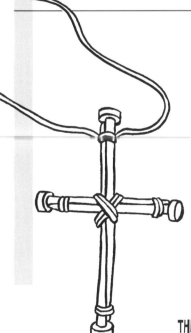

PRAISE WINDMILLS

Kids can tell others about Jesus with these fun conversation starters.

WHAT YOU'LL NEED:

You'll need sugar paper cut into squares roughly 23 cm wide, scissors, pins (with a round head), beads, pencils with erasers on top, additional small erasers.

FOR EXTRA IMPACT:

- Read aloud **Psalm 9:1**, and ask the children to talk about good things God has done in their lives.

- Ask the children to write the words of **Psalm 9:1** on a tag and attach it to their windmill with string as a reminder to praise the Lord.

WHAT TO DO

Give each child a square of sugar paper and scissors. Cut the paper from each corner towards the centre, leaving about 1.5 cm uncut in the middle. Get the children to pull every other outer point into the middle, then help them to push a straight pin through the centre to hold the paper points in the middle. They should put a bead on the pin behind the paper wheel. Then help them to push the pin into the eraser on a long pencil. (If it sticks out of the other end, attach another small eraser to avoid scratches.)

Say: one of the most exciting parts about knowing Jesus is being able to tell others about him. Who can you tell about Jesus? Suggest that the children give their windmills to these people as a way of starting up a conversation about Jesus.

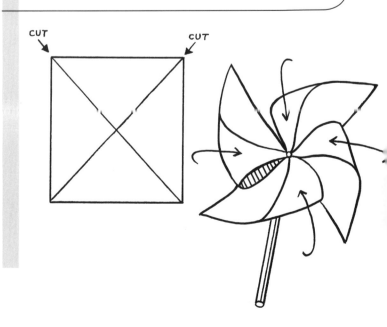

RAIN STICK

Kids love these gentle noisemakers.

WHAT YOU'LL NEED:

For each rain stick, you'll need 1 empty kitchen-towel tube, 70 g dry rice, glue, masking tape, a ruler, scissors and aluminium foil. You'll also need craft materials such as poster paint, beads, paintbrushes, feathers and glitter, and you will need a Bible.

FOR EXTRA IMPACT:

- Ask the children to take turns talking about promises they've made to others, and how it feels when people keep their promises.

- Children can choose a favourite song and together use their rain sticks as accompaniment instruments.

WHAT TO DO

Give each child two pieces of aluminium foil about one and a half times the length of the kitchen-towel tube and about 15 cm wide. Crunch the foil into two long, thin, snake-like shapes, and then twist each one into a spring shape and place in the tube. Cover one end of the tube with masking tape. Pour the rice in the tube. Cover the open end and secure it with masking tape.

Read aloud **Genesis 9:16**. Say: after God sent rains that flooded the earth, he promised never again to flood the earth. God created a rainbow so that whenever we see one, we'll remember God's promise.

Let the children use the craft materials to decorate their rain sticks with rainbows to remind them of God's promise in **Genesis 9:16**.

OLDER CHILDREN

SPLATTER PRINTS

Kids will learn that God can transform bad situations into something good.

WHAT YOU'LL NEED:

You'll need a Bible, an old salad spinner, paper, scissors, poster paint and paintbrushes.

FOR EXTRA IMPACT:

- If you don't have a salad spinner, use a shallow cardboard box. Place paper inside the box, drop splatters of paint on the paper and roll marbles on the paper.

- Fill plastic cups one quarter full of unpopped popcorn and stir in one spoonful of paint. Place one sheet of paper in the bottom of a shallow box, pour the paint-coated kernels on to the paper, and shake the box gently to create a design.

WHAT TO DO

One at a time, ask each child to cut a long, rectangular strip of paper and place it around the edge inside the salad-spinner basket. Then place dabs of paint on the paper, close the lid, and turn the handle. Open the spinner, take out the beautiful picture and show it to the group. Set it aside to dry.

Ask: which picture do you like the best—the one before or after it was changed?

Share a situation that God transformed in your life. Then say: talk about a bad thing that has happened to you or someone you know. How did God turn that bad thing into something good? Did you learn something through it?

Read aloud **Romans 8:28**. Say: the Bible says God can take the bad things in our lives and transform them into something good. God does this for us because he loves us and wants us to become more like Christ. Let's pray and thank God for the good he brings out of bad things.

SUMMER REPORTS

Kids celebrate all the great things that happened during the summer with this creative idea.

WHAT YOU'LL NEED:

You'll need a medium-size box and lid for each child, suitable magazines and catalogues, sugar paper, felt-tip pens, scissors and glue.

FOR EXTRA IMPACT:

- Take a photo of each child. Ask the children to glue their photo on to their box lid for a fun visible reminder of how they're changing throughout the year.

- Write a note of encouragement to each child to put in his or her box.

- Encourage the children to work together to make a group collage box for a fun time capsule. Put in a group photo and add other mementos throughout the year to enjoy revisiting at the year's end.

WHAT TO DO

Lay out magazines and catalogues, and let the children cut out or write phrases or words on sugar paper that describe things they did during the summer, such as a holiday, swimming or reading. Then ask them to cut out pictures that show the things they did, and glue them to their boxes.

As their boxes are drying, encourage the children to take turns describing their creations and their summer activities. Then let them take their boxes home and use them to store new school memories, such as favourite notes or crafts.

At the end of the school year, ask the children to bring their boxes back to church and share their memories.

OLDER CHILDREN

UNMASKED

Kids explore how to be honest with others.

WHAT YOU'LL NEED:

You'll need a Bible, A4 sheets of card, scissors, pencils, feathers, wool, tinsel, pipe cleaners, paint, paintbrushes, glue, elastic and a stapler.

FOR EXTRA IMPACT:

- Let the children have a fashion show and take turns modelling their masks.

- Ask the children to share things that make them afraid and want to hide behind a mask. Remind them that God sees our hearts and we have nothing to fear with him.

WHAT TO DO

Let the children cut their card into any shape they want to make their mask. They should cut out eyeholes and decorate the mask using the craft materials. Measure out a length of elastic that will fit around each child's head. Staple the elastic piece to each side of the mask. Encourage the children to wear their masks.

Ask: why do people wear masks? What purpose does a mask serve? What kind of imaginary masks can people wear to hide who they really are? What do you think God thinks of people wearing these imaginary masks?

Read aloud **1 John 1:5–7**. Ask: how is wearing a mask like walking in the darkness? What does it mean to walk in the light? Why do some people try to hide who they are by walking in the darkness? How can we be more honest with each other? How can we continue to walk in the light?

Close in prayer, asking for God's help to walk in the light and be honest with each other.

OLDER CHILDREN

SCRIPTURE INDEX: OLD TESTAMENT

SCRIPTURE INDEX: NEW TESTAMENT

INDEX

SEASONAL INDEX

ALSO FROM BRF:

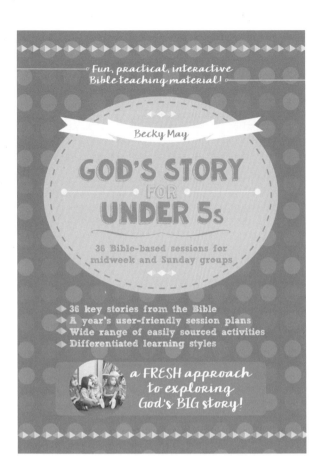

LET'S SHARE GOD'S BIG STORY!

Use as a year-long weekly programme or dip in and out to highlight individual stories at key times of year and supplement other activities.

Varied storytelling methods enable children to engage with God's big story in different ways, with a range of activities to illustrate and explore the story, catering for different learning preferences and using materials that most children's groups will already have to hand.

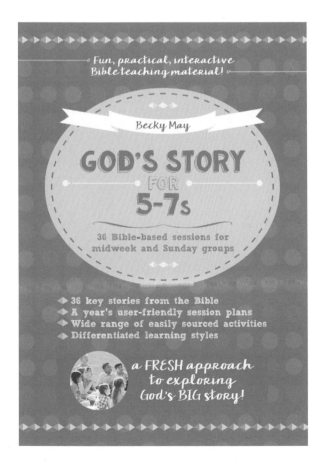

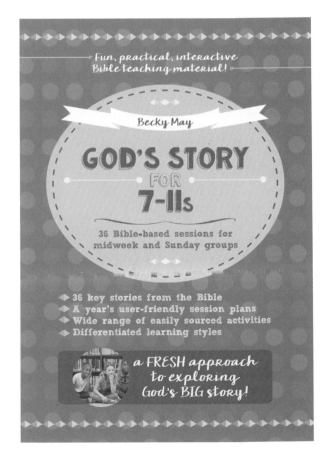